Daughter of the Razor

An Australian true crime story

Maria Tinschert

Published in 2016 by Maria Tinschert

Published with the assistance of Publicious Pty Ltd

Typesetting by:
Publicious Pty Ltd
www.publicious.com.au

Cover design by: Joe-Anne Kek-Pamenter
jo@jusjocreative.com.au

Catalogue-in-Publication details available
from the National Library of Australia

ISBN: 978-0-9953977-0-5 (print)
Copyright © Maria Tinschert 2016
Non-fiction — Biography

As I stand by the dark silent water
The night a mantel of black velvet I wear
Gazing up at the crystal stars shining
Feeling the touch of night air
My heart has a song of its own now
Not the same as it was as a girl
Whose thoughts had been poisoned and twisted
Days and nights filled with torture and pain
It was a little life wasted
A voice never heard
But your aching heart and childlike soul
Have to learn where to put your trust
My heart has a song of its own now
Not the same as it was as a girl
It's a song of pride and dignity
It's called survival
And that in itself is a pearl.
The day mum forgot me a little
The day mum forgot me a lot
The doctor who told,
I wish she could see what I got.
It is in life love is needed
Because in death there is nothing to feel
Save your tears, my family of weakness
Bottle them to put on a shelf
For the day will come
When you will need them for yourself.

Acknowledgements

I dedicate this book to all those who think there is no hope, so they may learn from me. While you live, there is hope and it's never too late for an Angel to find you, like she found me.

In a little corner of the Elanora Library, she was a pretty little young woman with long blonde hair and a tender smile. She didn't have wings and fly over me, but I knew that even without wings she was that Angel and was there for me. She fills a place in my heart and just like me, you will know it when your Angel finds you.

Little Mary

Foreword by Ralph James

The book you are about to read is a shocking story in itself – but is an even greater story of survival. I have known Maria Tinschert for more than twenty years. I didn't know little Mary, the wretched character described in most of the pages of this book. I have never before read a non-fiction account of such depravity, such sadism and such debauchery. And all inflicted on the same girl, the same adolescent and the same woman, by the very people she ought to have been able to depend on to protect her.

Maria's survival and her metamorphose from Mary to Maria is an inspirational as it is tragic. The physical pain she endured is matched only by what must be a deep emotional and psychological legacy.

Before moving on to a more sedate area of the law, I had been a criminal lawyer for approaching 30 years. I specialised in criminal defence and had been accredited as a specialist in that field. In my contact with people who the law calls defendants, accused, offenders, prisoners and victims I have never met any single person who has been subjected to the level of evil you will read about. More importantly, I have never encountered any victim who has survived so much and who has emerged triumphant to go on and accomplish so much.

In practice I have represented women charged with murder who have killed a violent partner after having endured years of physical and emotional abuse. Battered woman syndrome has been recognised by the law with increasing acceptance. I don't seek to diminish the suffering of other victims but none of the women I have acted for suffered to the same degree as did Maria.

Many years ago, Maria on behalf of the Tinschert family presented me with a plaque which I proudly displayed at the entry to my office. It reads:

To a lawyer among lawyers, Ralph James – Many thanks, many times for his skilled, persistent and courageous fight for justice for those, who without him, would have no voice against man's inhumanity to man. The Tinscherts.

Until I read Maria's book I did not fully appreciate what she meant by "no voice against man's inhumanity to man." Given that she experienced "man's inhumanity to man" first hand, and to the highest degree, I am every more proud to know, after reading her book, the esteem in which she holds me and that she has for the work I did.

What the following pages describe is not just man's inhumanity to man, but the absolute powerlessness young Mary experienced and the total lack of a voice from anyone, anywhere, to relieve her of her plight.

Ralph James Solicitor
Accredited Specialist - Criminal Law

CHAPTER ONE

Mary Josephine Goodfield was my name and I was born on the 6th of August, 1932. My father was an English Jew from Leeds, Yorkshire England, aged 33 years at the time of my birth. He was a labourer.

My mother was an Australian by birth, once widowed, and also 33 years old at the time of my birth. I was the last living child and the only female born to my mother after the birth of six sons, three of whom were conceived and born prior to her marriage to my father. One son was from her previous husband and two others were from what she described as affairs.

I was born at 19 Sherbrooke Lane, East Sydney, in the front room of the little house. At approximately four years of age I moved with my family to Chullora, where I lived with them for approximately 11 years.

'Daughter of the Razor' is the story of a child who would remain locked in fear until old age, following the violence of child prostitution, sexual tortures, murder and the terror of being locked in a closet day after day.

The critics will say this book is the work of an amateur and, of course, they are right. But they must realize, and this is the point, that this book was written by the grown-up Mary who never had enough schooling or loving. It is written because I wanted to show other survivors that you can survive, you can grow, and that it's never too late.

I will probably never be famous for my writing, but I may be

19 Sherbrook Lane where I was born   **2011 returning to Sherbrook Lane**

famous for the story of how I survived because you see, 70 years later I am still here. I have confronted my pain and written of it for others the victims, believers, non-believers and, of course, for the abusers. They didn't win — I won!

I need to caution readers that my experiences told here may be extremely disturbing to some. This story is violent and graphic and could be upsetting to read. But it is true and must be told the way it really happened, whether it makes people uncomfortable or not. My story, and others like it, will help people to come forward. With the impact of its horror coupled with the fact that this story is a true account of events that happened in this country we, the survivors can help to prevent it from continuing to happen. Exposure will help to stop abuse.

As you read through this book, you will see where I have repeated myself. Of course, no real writer would dare do that — but I hope my editor leaves my repeats in, because it is not so much that I tell the same story more than once, rather it is because it has impact. In my world of pain I found that sometimes just saying it again was relief in a way, once I had learned how to talk about some things that hurt so much. I feel sure other survivors will agree with me. I suppose it's because you live for so long in silence that it's like pressure lifting each time you speak. So if you come across my repeats, hang in there. Just read on and try to prevent repeats of my life happening to any other person. That is why I have let you look into my private world of sadness. It's not just for me, you know.

I do not believe that it's possible to be totally healed from the horror of sexual or violent abuse, but I believe that you can go on to succeed in life. Because victims are much stronger than most people. The title 'survivor' says it all. We learn very early how to look fine while carrying the weight of a ton of bricks on our back. But beware, there are inexperienced people who want us all to put it all behind us and move on. This is very wrong.

How can you put something behind you when you cannot even look at it and when your mind wants to say it didn't happen? When you can say "I am the victim, I am not guilty." They are the criminals, "I am innocent" Only then will your steps become lighter. Because then you have put the weight of guilt where it belongs. I don't believe you put it behind you, I believe you put it in its right place. This allows you to go on, and to succeed in life because you have taken over from the power of others, and from the guilt they forced upon you so that they would always be sure of your silence.

It had been a quiet day, oppressively hot, the air still, as if a storm was coming, when my telephone rang and a woman spoke.

"It's Pamela here."

"Pamela who?"

"You know who it is 'Pamela Stonson'. Meet me in front of the Medical Centre at Kippa-ring Village at 4 o'clock with $100."

I knew Pamela Stonson as a customer, when we owned an antique shop. I'd bought some goods from her after she'd told me a sad story about wanting to get away from a brutal husband and save her little girl. I had even been to her home in the past and brought goods to help her out and she showed me scars on her body from being battered by her husband. (Although I later found out that the scars were from kidney surgery when she was a child.)

I hadn't heard from her since and now I didn't believe what I was hearing. 'You must be joking. Why?'

"Because I said so, you bitch. You've got plenty, you and all your diamonds. We know where you live so be there or we'll come and kill you."

I rang the Redcliffe police who told me to come down to the station in case the house was being watched. I showed them my second-hand dealer's licence and described what had happened. They told me to go ahead with the meeting, they then wired me up with a recorder, and assured me I'd be safe as they would be hiding in the car park.

Pamela Stonson approached me outside the medical centre. "Have you got the money?"

"How dare you ring me and make such a demand. "No," I said, starting to move back to the car. I was nervous by then.

As I got near the car she started to scream and lunged at me with a weapon. Before she could plunge it into my stomach, the detectives appeared, identified themselves and brought her under control by lifting her off the ground. They arrested her. At the station I learned she had, a letter opener in her hand.

No one realised the impact of this event on me. But I was not treated as a victim, just as a lucky old woman. Even my family said, "Wow, lucky you, mum, she didn't stab you, just forget it". "Thank God you're OK."

But this was not the way I felt! This woman had wanted to hurt me. She was just like my mother, my mother-in-law, the nuns who closed their eyes to a little girl's pain, my father and the men who used, abused and treated me worse than any animal should ever been treated. In that moment I knew Pamela Stonson's attack was the last violent act my poor tortured mind could take. In the past when someone had hurt me I would justify it in my mind. This time I could not.

When I got hit, insulted or abused in any way at all, I would tell myself it was my fault. I was conditioned to feeling guilty for creating all the terrible things that were done to me. I'd been told it was my own fault that things happened to me and I lived by this rule. This time I wanted to know why this terrible thing had happened. What had I done? Should I take the blame? This woman was in her early thirties, about the same age as my youngest child. What had I done to her? I was not her mother. What gave her the right to put demands on me? Why?

My mind kept tossing it around in fear of punishment for telling the police. This was something I'd not done before and it was very disturbing.

When I rang the police station a couple of days later they informed me Pamela Stonson was not in jail like they said she would be. They did not appear to be upset about this. But this time I was — I was shocked.

Every few days I rang the detective to ask if she was in jail again. But it never happened. This event turned my life upside down. I could no longer go near the shops where the incident occurred in case she was there as she was out on bail. I lived almost opposite the shopping centre but would drive to a smaller centre in another district. My nice little home where we had chosen to live had become the scene of a living nightmare for me. Eventually we had to sell up and move. It was obvious something had happened to me. I was no longer justifying what had happened to me. I'd seen enough of other people's violence and no longer wanted to be the victim.

After the incident one of the detectives was very persistent and notified Victims of Crime and shortly after I found myself in the capable hands of a trauma counselor in the Valley in Brisbane. I would like to thank the Redcliff Police for their help and consideration in referring the Victims of Crime Counselor to me. If it wasn't for this I would never off talked.

Upon meeting my counselor, it was immediately clear to me I had met someone with extreme insight into the world of the victim. It's a world that many of professionals I'd met before had not been able to enter.

At the beginning it had felt all right because I was an expert at covering up and saying only what I wanted people to hear. But then she started to dig a little. This made me want to get out of there.

What gave this woman the right to step across my boundaries? I was OK. Pamela Stonson had tried to stab me and I was a little upset, nothing more. I could handle it. I always handled things, didn't I?

I decided I would not be coming back to see the counsellor. That would be enough for me. The only trouble was she seemed to a very nice person so it was going to be hard to tell her that I wasn't coming back. But that's what I wanted. I didn't want to get involved in this sort of thing. If the police hadn't told her about me, this event would have passed like everything else. I was not going to get sucked in, not if I could help it. Those were my real thoughts and feelings about this therapist.

But I did continue and I started to see her as often as I could. She had started to show me not only shadows but light. She was for real. This counsellor understood things that I didn't, especially things about me. I was allowing her to see me in ways I had never allowed anybody else to see me. Little by little I was peeping out from the closet. This was scary, but she was always there. She warned me it wasn't going to be easy, and that it would not be without pain. She knew what she was talking about.

Some days I would come out of my shell quite a long way, and other times it was too much to even think about. Even though my thoughts occupied a terrible place to be, I was used to being there. I even felt secure there as nobody could see my pain there in the dark. She would help me to come out again to the point where it started to become a habit. She was showing me that I could live and breathe outside of the closet if I was willing to try. Soon I found I wanted to see my counsellor as often as possible and another fear crept in. I was becoming dependent on my therapist. Hell! I was going from bad to worse.

I also began to fear she would go away and I would be alone again, and worse than that, I would be alone outside of the closet with only the horrible things in my life in front of me again. What should I do?

It occurred to me that I should go back to the way I had been before. At least I could survive that way. It was my way where I was not in danger of becoming dependent on anyone. But now I'd learned to trust another female and I never expected this. She was very different from me but she knew me. All of that made me decide that I should go back into the closet. I felt lost, and confused about being dependent on her, stirred up by the pain of confrontation.

But I knew I couldn't just retreat without being honest with her. I had to ring and tell her the truth because she deserved it. She had been honest and straight with me. She had never mollycoddled me or pampered me as others might have done under similar circumstances. She deserved my truth.

When I told her of my decision, I knew she cared but she also knew it was the way I had to do it and that she respected my decision. So I went back into the closet and planned to push everything back into place as it had been before therapy. But I found that I could not push things back to where they were before.

I began to see that I would not become dependent on her, and that I could trust her. I also realized that I could learn coping skills from her that had not been available to me before. Now there was a chance for me to live in a new way that allowed me to be myself without shame, without loss of dignity, not as a slave to the will of others, but as a woman.

Three months after leaving I sent her a Christmas card. It was special. She understood. She is truly a counsellor of great skill. When she read the card she knew I was ready to return to therapy and she rang me.

I started to move out of the closet again but it took a year or more to commence making notes. She had urged me to try to write but until now it had not seemed possible. But this time, as I looked at myself. I could see the changes. I knew she was right, and wished I had started to write much earlier.

If you are feeling angry about what has happened to you and are not ready to talk about it, you can try to write about it. Writing can help to ease the pain. It helps, and for me it started one day when I'd been really hurt. I felt that I had been born just to be hurt and I was unwell in the strangest way, very mixed up, so I got myself a notebook and hid it in a briefcase with a lock. I did not want anybody reading this stuff, not even my second husband. It was not because he would intrude, it was that I didn't trust anyone. How could I? Why should I?

Anyway there I was with my hiding place and notepad ready. I sat down at the table, with the TV switched on and a cup of tea next to me, and what do you think I thought of? Nothing! Blank! Zilch! So I watched TV and thought what a stupid idea! Write what? Then the penny dropped, I'll write that, 'It's a stupid idea'. So that's what happened. I wrote it and then added how I felt at that moment plus what else cheesed me off. It meant I had started, just like that.

Then I noticed that I was starting to think how much I hated my abusers, and then why I hated them.

It just spread and I wrote and wrote. I was doing something so powerful, it was unbelievable to me that I could do that. After all, didn't I know that telling could bring more trouble?

I am very articulate. I'd like to say I'm proud of myself for having the courage to write this book. It is one hell of a step forward for me, just knowing that I did it. I came out of the closet once and for all, and found another special thing in my life — my wonderful feelings. I now have many of them, and they are not just good or bad ones.

My counselor has shown me that she is proud of me and this

is important, but she should also be proud of herself because I am what I am through her generosity, care and skill, and because she did not give up on me. I was able to put this shocking story on paper so please don't put this book down now because it doesn't have the feel of a bestseller or a masterpiece of literature, as you will be wrong. It is a book you must read and you must try to see that others read it, too, because it's like the brakes in your car — you don't need them while you're driving, but if you wanted to stop you must have them or someone may lose their life and it could be you, or one of yours.

This book will help to prevent someone killing another and help to prevent another Mary suffering years of pain and torment because nobody wanted to see or hear her.

When I look back at myself as a little girl I see a sad sight. It fills me with pain for the little girl who seemed to be always alone and on the brink of death. Her sweet little life was so close to ending many times, but for reasons too hard to understand, I did not go to my grave. Even though my childhood died and the little girl in me grew into forced womanhood, I went on.

It's hard at times to look at the violence and silence that surrounded me without thinking that somebody should have seen the telltale signs; somebody should have listened to me, even though the words were unspoken for most of my life. This world seems to have many clever people — doctors, police, teachers — so how is it possible that nobody helped me?

Why was I overlooked by society? What is wrong? Is it because we are supposed to be a minority group of people or is it that people don't want to be bothered and don't want to get involved? Will it go away if we ignore it, and look; it's on TV all the time now, so how do you know if it is happening to somebody if they don't tell?

My answer to my own questions is to start looking for signs and don't kid yourself it couldn't happen in your own beautiful family. There is a big chance that it is and has been going on for a long time. And also, don't think that it could only be the guy next door who is scruffy or looks a bit different to you. And don't always judge the male. The pretty lady with the dear little child is just as likely to be an abuser as the man, and she will have a better chance of getting away with it. Unfortunately, we do judge books and people by their covers and this is our biggest mistake.

CHAPTER TWO

The Goodfields, Brookfields, Valencia Street, Chullora was written on the letters that came to my house. It sounded better than it was.

There was no electricity, of course. We used lamps and candles, mainly for light, a wood copper to wash the clothes in and to heat water for a bath, a fuel stove in the centre of the house with irons to heat on the stove, three bedrooms, with a living area a front verandah and a back verandah. That house was hell encased in wood in a yard with a wire fence.

The day we moved to Chullora my mother made her position clear to my father. She walked up onto the verandah and smashed her fist through the front window and screamed at him:

"If you think I'll stay out here you fucking bastard, you're wrong. You won't keep me out here in the bush just for you and them bastards, you're not good enough."

She was right. It was dirty and dusty, with no real roads, just tracks full of potholes and dry in the heat of summer, and full of mud and slush in the rains of winter. If you walked through the scrub for a distance you came to a shop owned by people named Phillis. They sold all the things you might need in the back of nowhere. It was a good shop. Then we had another shop owned by a Mrs. Gibson and a big shed for the local bus depot. After walking to the shop through the bush, you caught the bus to Punchbowl or Bankstown and the old train to the 'Big Smoke'.

The street where we lived had a beautiful name for an ugly

place. There were only five or so houses in the street amid scrub that hid so many other ugly things, like the man who liked to walk through the bush with his pants undone and show anybody his penis. Nobody ever put a stop to that.

We had bad bushfires regularly and experienced many days of heat wave conditions. It sure was hell in every sense of the word and the house being wood was like a bomb ready to go off. Every fire was a threat to us, but sometimes I would have liked it to burn in my child's mind, and maybe my poor life would have taken another turn. The bush also gave protection when the men came to play the Swy, better known as two-up, at the back of our place. My parents loved it because when the police raided them. Everybody ran in all directions in the dark and left beer, money, anything. They had to get away from the law and my parents got the stuff they left behind.

Because we had no electricity and our only radio was battery operated, my father only turned on the radio to hear a programme from Long Bay Jail that was put on by the prisoners. It was music. The other programme was called 'Nancy the Witch and Her Cat Salem'. I never heard all of these programmes because I was allowed such a liberty for only a short time. The batteries were special.

The bed I slept in was made of rough and itchy chaff bags and the base or frame was made of wood and full of smelly fat bed bugs. I don't know if many children slept like this, but I'm not complaining. I just want it to be known as part of the background of myself, there were people that had mattresses, sheets and blankets but not for me.

Every day was a nightmare for me as a child in that house. Sometimes I pretended I was a dog because the dog got left alone and I too wanted to be left alone, free of the paralysis of fear. Even being on a chain was painless compared to some of the things thought up for me by my mother. I remember one morning after the boys and my father left, she had a tin dish in the bedroom to use as a toilet because ours was out back in the yard and they never went there in the night. She spilt some as she carried it out. When she slopped it up from the floor with a cloth, she stuffed the urine soaked rag into my mouth and made me leave it there till she pulled it out much later.

There was always something vile in her head that she liked to torture me with. It seemed to give her pleasure. When we were alone her name for me was 'Jew bastard'. It took me years to understand why and what it meant. It didn't matter anyway because I was insulted without knowing what it was all about. They called me 'hook nose' when I got older and developed features like a little Jewess, 'spindle legs', 'ugly', 'shit-head', 'bitch', 'slut', 'cunt'. It was just a way of life, those names, but today it hurts — the impact of those injuries goes on. I guess it's because I now understand the real degradation.

Another fun thing for my mother was bad temper. She appeared to like it. Many of her soup bowls she would smash on my head. Holding them in both hands she would 'crown me'. She said, "I would be known forever as Jew bastard". I think the only reason she stopped using dishes was because she would have to buy more and I wasn't worth that. In fact, in her eyes, I didn't appear to be worth anything.

One very hot day, I made the mistake of asking my mother for a drink of water when she was lying down. She was so angry, she actually did get off the bed and got a glass of water which she then held in her hand and pushed into my mouth till the glass broke and cut my mouth. The stinging was awful, but it only seemed to make her angrier. Then she got an old enamel mug, filled it with water and made me drink till it started to pour back out of my mouth. She did this about half a dozen times. My stomach hurt very much and she told me that next time I asked for water she would put my head in a bucket of it. So I didn't ask ever again.

My life was made up of violent experiences, most but not all at the hands of my mother. As a child I had no idea of what mothers were supposed to be like, but inside me was the feeling that she was good and it was my fault she did things to me that hurt. If I could be better she wouldn't have to hurt me; it was my fault she drank plonk, and it was my fault she was angry. I would do anything to make her like me, such as bending right over so that she could easily kick me. She liked to do that because when she kicked me I would bounce in the air a bit and she would do it more to see how high she could get me. As she did so she would say, 'Isn't this fun? Aren't we having a good time?' I would have to say "yes". But the odd thing is I didn't mind what she did because I wanted her to like me and she seemed to like me then.

Of course, even a child's mind starts to wake up that something is wrong, and violence begins to take on a new meaning. I didn't understand, but I accepted that this was the way it was going to be in that house. There would be no saviour. It was to be my prison and the rooms became the torture chambers.

Each room was to play a part in my life. The cupboard, or wardrobe in the front room was my own private chamber of hell where only the black eyes of darkness watched me in silence and felt my fear. The smell is still with me today, sometimes enough to make me want to scream out or be sick, or rush away. It will not go away. They were terrible times, at least five or six times a week or more. It always depended on her or at least her needs. Once I was in that wardrobe that was that and, when she locked that door, fear settled in. It was icy fear, the type that twisted your thoughts.

The heat in there was vile and it smelt of my brother's stinky shoes. I could hear my heart beating loudly when I was in there. I hoped that somebody would hear it and help me, but, of course, nobody ever heard it. Now I guess I should mention that stuffing my mouth full of bread was their way of silencing me and at the same time, if I died, they had the story ready for the police that I loved eating bread and choked to death on it. The bread bulged out my mouth and was stuffed up my nose so that it felt as if I couldn't breathe. At least this was what my father said and believed.

My mother was always covering herself against future problems. She would say to me, 'You know Mad Willie? Well, he's your daddy's uncle and you are just like him, but I won't tell anybody if you don't. You know you can trust your mum, don't you?' The threat was always there that if I talked, at the very least I would be sent to a mad house, or the mental institution, or locked in a dungeon, forever always laying in blood with no light, and no food. She was skilled at being a clever monster and I was afraid of her. Always after this type of talk she made me masturbate her. She would first give me a washout with her big red and black pump thing with a tube on it. Then afterwards when I was still shaking, she would take her floral housecoat off and lie down naked on the lino floor with a pillow under her bottom where she would remain until it was over. Then she would have a drink from a bottle that she kept hidden under the house, so that Dad wouldn't drink it.

It was just a normal day in this little girl's life. And pain that was a part of that every day life; walking in pain; sleeping in pain and the pain when I was very hurt inside me by my father. I didn't know what he did, just that when he put his penis in me, my mother had made him put some sticky stuff on me first. I don't know what it was, but I think now that it was Vaseline or stuff like that. Whatever it was it didn't help me. He had put bread in my mouth, but still I could feel screaming inside me. The hurting just did not stop. After he pulled away from me, she looked up inside me and said, 'Christ, now look what you did. I've got to fix her up a bit.' And she did, with cotton dipped in iodine and a fine needle. She said 'One stitch, that's all.' And still I wear the scar, along with many others.

I know this story goes on in such a horrific way it never ends, it really never ends you know. The funny things is when you live with murder over your head, it's like I don't know how to explain that really. My mother, father or my brothers could have of killed me I know it sounds ludicrous but back then that wasn't ludicrous. All they had to do was close ranks and they could of said it was death by misadventure or something, many things they could of said, many things could have happened but here I am and it didn't happen but there was so much, so much to the horror of these people.

I have been asked or told that I have a right to judge her my mother, but I don't because after all she was my mother. I did nestle in her womb for nine months and on the 6th day of August 1932, just like any other woman she felt pains of birth and delivered a healthy baby girl and called her Mary. Perhaps it was only for a short time but she was just like any other mother, even the mother of Jesus, who I'm told gave birth to her child the same way. These are things that you do think about and what was this woman really like in my eyes what did I really think? Well I thought she was so beautiful and she had lovely legs, beautiful black curly hair, creamy skin, dark eyes that flashed, a magnificent figure, good feet and a lot of power. She knew what she wanted and did not allow anything or anyone to stand in her way, "children were things you had when the crochet hook and soap pencil failed" she always said. "God created the world OK but he gave power to men and slavery to women, who for the most part have no idea how to use their power which was strong by far", she said. She also said "for a female it was better to be known as a killer than to be known as a slave".

My mother had black hair and a heart to match, she had bathing rituals and they were just that a 'ritual'. Cleanliness was a must, that was a must for her, soap, water, perfume and a mirror and she was happy. She didn't care much about other people or their comfort because as she said she wasn't a slave, she lived the way she wanted to live and did what she wanted to do. People were just puppets to her, you threw them away when you were finished with them because as she said she hated men including her own lot and she meant it. She also used to say woman were even worse, she would have slashed or killed anyone who stood in her way I think and if I had followed in her footsteps she would have liked that.

But instead of following her way, I chose the opposite way so that meant she would never say she cared about me. She pumped evil into me but I pushed it out the other side. In her eyes I was a useless person and the story takes a funny twist because years later I studied with the Salvation Army to become a community care minister to help people, to help people wherever they were.

My wish was to serve in a way that I surely understood, I have been non-forgiving for those years, yet I dedicated my life for others. By others I meant the ones that didn't get looked after like that by the Salvation Army. See, I have my own views, my own beliefs and my own experiences with them, so I thought if I become one than I'll be a good one, not like them, not a hypocrite.

CHAPTER THREE

Among the many sickening things they did to me was the hanging one. I really hated it. My mother and father enjoyed watching me hang from the wardrobe. My father made a frame out of wood, a bit like a crucifix with rope loops hanging from the arms and a thing like a butcher's hook from the centre. That went over the wardrobe. They would put a dish on the floor under it, then take my clothes off, strap me onto the frame, put the loops over my legs and fix me onto the top of the wardrobe. They would pull the loops, my legs would bend up.

They would lay on the bed naked, playing, as she called it, telling me 'don't pee till I tell you and then you can come down.' Sometimes it seemed like I was hanging forever while they played with each other. Then, if they were finished, she would tell me to pee and it had to go into the dish. I learned to do it very slowly; no matter if I wanted to do it fast. That was one hell of a thing to go through, but it was only one of many that she thought up. I also remember there were times when she would put her scanties on me. They were so big and with big wide legs. God, I must have looked a terrible sight, but they each must have loved it. They laughed and seemed to like me looking like that. My mother always seemed to be comparing her adult body with my child's body. She shaved all her body hair off and then asked my father which one looked the best — hers or mine?

If kids could hide from the bogeyman, what could I do? I was the bogeyman's daughter. When I was in this terrible childhood drama, the thought of telling was in and out like the tide until there were no thoughts at all. And it's not a case now of being believed; it's a case of talking about it and relieving a little of the lonely agony of those memories. Each time my father beat me it was my head he went for, or sometimes the soles of my feet. He left marks, but who could see? He always looked like he was in another world, a happy one for him. X-rays showed that there were bones broken in my feet, but never attended to. 'Your daddy needs this because he's only got mummy, you know.' How those words now make me sick. 'Poor Daddy, look at how big his tool has got and it needs work. If you're a good girl you will open your legs wide and then daddy can work his tool.' I always did what I was told, no matter how painful.

I'll help end child abuse by telling my story and breaking the silence in which it thrives. I hope to be a model for other victims. When my father was being violent to my mother, he would always yell at her: "I am the man, not you. Remember that, I am the man." I think now he was trying to convince himself of this fact, not her, because she was the man and she was the woman; she was the devil and he was the bogeyman.

Sometimes I liked being in the pen with the dog. It was hot, but quiet in there. The dog was on the chain and couldn't get back to me. The fence was too high for me to get out. I suppose it was the right place for me at the time; at least while I was in there she left me alone.

As you will see when you read on, I was to suffer many injuries and among them are the phobias and fears. Also because of many things my mouth is another very big problem. My teeth had all rotted off, but the roots remained and I cannot have anyone put their hand or anything else in my mouth for more than a moment. So dentistry, as such, was out of the question; also blood, especially mine.

However, I did find a dental mechanic who made dentures for my mouth to fit over my own roots and broken teeth. He took impressions in a few moments with my own assistance and hence

I have a reasonable looking mouth with teeth. They are not very comfortable or good for eating with, but it put me up front with society and I looked just like everybody else.

Just recently though, my therapist told me that combining a new technique from America for trauma victims, plus the assistance of a doctor and dentist working altogether, may give me a chance of a future with a mouth that really works; meaning not just talks, but eats as well, so I have my fingers crossed. Really it would be so nice to try foods that you chew, not just swallow.

When you meet somebody you would never tell them your sad secret and even after months or even years of friendship. You might say that it wasn't the best childhood, but you would say it in such a way that it never went further. Even non-abused people have a sort of code about certain things we can and cannot talk about and like. It is an unwritten law that you must speak well of your parents, and if you speak badly about brothers or sisters, it's because you're immature or jealous. This is why a victim stays a victim for so long. How can you tell? When can you tell? And most of all, who can you tell? Abuse will end when a person can tell other people.

Abusers live on lies and hate the truth; when the truth comes out, they might go in. It has been very hard for me to try to put the right year with the right incident. This is not uncommon in cases like mine when there are no birthdays or celebrations to associate with time or dates. So I will say it is just before I went to school, after I had started school, before marriage, after marriage, before death, after death. I've done my very best to be accurate and left out anything that my mind and memories were in doubt about. By doing this, I will be able to focus on the truth.

I would like to say that as much as I can never forgive my family or understand their actions, I cannot write about many other incidents that took place because of the doubts of accuracy in my mind. I will not, therefore, stoop to lies in order to paint an even worse picture of them than they did themselves. There have been many times I have wished them to hell and back, but I won't become as vile as they are. I am me and I am different. I didn't die for them and I won't lie for them, but they made me hate my body and that is really bad.

I didn't like my own blood and I still don't, but it's getting a little better, as I get older and more confident of myself. But memories are very disturbing sometimes, such as my memories of my father. To me my father was a smelly man with hair. He was the bogeyman and I was the bogeyman's daughter, so how could I hide. I hated him squashing me, but my mother liked it.

The pain is always there each day. Something reminds me and it hurts. I wish it had never happened. Blood, pain, shame, anger, loss, fear — hell, I want love; I want what I deserve. I feel sad and hurt with the world.

All of my young life I was in pain from the waist down, never free of it. My back passage always bleeding; my front always stinging, burning pain; my pants nearly always had blood in them, though I don't think I got my periods until I was about 13 years old. My life continued along these lines — lots of anal-tearing; bowel trouble, vaginal problems; cancer of the uterus; a little bone here (my war medals), a little scar there. Who will see them? (And who cares anyway?)

Another one of my mother's pet likes was to make me stand in the corner with a piece of wood, about as long as a school ruler, between my legs and no clothes on. If I dropped it the time would start all over again.

Sometimes it went on till midday. There was never anyone for me. I was always on my own and if only I had someone whom I could turn to, my brothers, a sister, aunties or anybody, I would not have had to go through this rotten stuff again. My brothers were brothers by flesh only, they were sexual predators and trainees of my parents. If somebody had just cared it would not have been allowed to happen. The only family I had were all abusers. I fully understand now, as a survivor, that my family used their power as adults, and my fear of them, to gratify their own depraved needs.

Just their size alone gave them power. But I am grown up now; I have the size and the power. It's not revenge that will help all victims. It's telling the truth at last without fear. However, if it makes you feel better, call it revenge.

Now another moment in my life was when my mother and father had a big fight and he walked out. He did not return that night, but in the morning Campsie Police let her know they had him in a cell at the station. He had been arrested for something or other and they would hold him until the court was held. So she took me with her to Campsie and while she was allowed to talk to him somewhere in the station, I was not. The policeman said it was not good for me. I waited outside and a kind policeman gave me a sandwich and milk. I sat and waited till my father was taken into court, then released to walk home with my mother and me. It was a good moment for me.

My father had been punished and my mother punished him more all the way home. After we arrived home she told him he was not worth her time because he could have brought big trouble onto them both. She never let him forget what he had done. She said it was bad to get mixed up with the police. Now as an adult, I can understand why she was worried.

By this time it must have been near Christmas because one morning my mother said 'Santa Claus has been' and I got a cane pram with a doll in it. But the trick was I wasn't allowed to play with it. I could push it around the house and out the front for our neighbours to see. That was that and it all came undone when I was standing out the front near the gate, watching the children up the street with their mums. They had all come together in front of the Smith's house. The next moment Lorna Smith called out to me, "Mary, come up and show us your dolly." I thought this was really Christmas. Some nice people had noticed I had a present. So up I pushed my pram and doll. When I got to them I could see the other children cuddling their toys, dolls and things. Lorna and the ladies said nice things to me, too. Then Lorna reached into the pram to take the doll out for further admiration and suddenly said, 'Christ, the cruel bastard has tied the doll down, so the poor kid can only look at it. But don't touch.' That started a whole new conversation with the ladies of Valencia Street. At that moment my mother spotted me and called me back.

Christmas was over for me. Going out the front I had learned a lesson, she made sure of that, but the boys were more conniving than me by far. They knew what she should see and what she shouldn't see. I really never learned how to be as smart as them, until now. But I survived. I remember when my father got council work. It was just what she wanted. He only worked part of the time and when he did she took me with her to East Sydney where she had a room in a house. There she also took her clients whom she picked up from anywhere or sometimes from the Wine Bar at Central Station. She would either leave me on the street or take me with her and make extra money with me. I was eight, nine or 10. These were bad days for me but good days for her.

My father did know of her prostitution racket with me. The only thing he didn't like was her being with her old friends from where we lived before. When she took me it made her look respectable, mother and daughter together. Shopping days, I suppose they thought, even though I should have been at school. I think she only sent me to school sometimes so as the Welfare wouldn't step in. I knew why they would never let me go to school more than a few days at a time because if I went longer and formed friendships, I might talk. They were always on their guard.

My mother didn't always take me with her to East Sydney. Lots of times she would go to her favourite wine bar at Central Station near the ramp. She would stand me outside till she picked me up. That could be anytime between during the morning and going home in the afternoon. She liked her wine and I know she drank a lot, but strangely enough I don't remember her ever staggering or looking drunk. My mother never came out to see if I was still there or wanted to go to the toilet or if I was hungry. This was her time, not mine. A couple of times she came out and started walking up to the station without even looking at me. I knew she had forgotten I was there, so I ran after her. She was surprised and glad I had chased her, but no caring look or smile.

She always carried a small but neat little suitcase, grey in colour and rather smart. Each time we went into the city, this is what she carried her wine in. My father hated her when she hid a bottle and didn't share it with him. She did it all the time, probably because once it was gone it was a long way to the hotel or wine bar to get another. So she would always bring a bottle or two home in the grey suitcase, each time we were in the city. Then she would hide them everywhere — under the house, in the bush, under her plants in the garden where she grew gladioli and chrysanthemums for me to take to the nuns so they would turn their backs.

What she also did was eat onions to hide the smell of the grog, but because she did it all the time, he knew why and when he smelt the onions, it was on again. She would look him square in the eye and lie till he hit her. Of course, this was pretty regular for a woman so tough. He was so tough, he could beat her up and she came home to him each time even though she had the other place and friends to go to and men by the dozen because she was a good looking woman with a perfect figure and lovely legs.

However, one day he snapped her arm like a thin piece of wood. For a long time I went with her to the Western Suburbs Hospital for treatment. She never told them how it happened — silence is the name of the game, remember — but as they took one plaster off after another, they had to put another back on.

She was just waiting to get back at him, that I knew, and I bet he knew it, too. Well, she got him all right. I saw her pour half a cup of Epsom salts into a bottle and then some wine. Later one day she let him find the bottle and made a big fuss about him going to drink it all, which he did. For some reason or other he went to Punchbowl and became very ill near the station. A lady got an ambulance, but my father refused to get in it. When he got home and told the story, he promised her she was in trouble later. So it went on all the time, fights and threats. She never changed, he never changed and my life never changed.

It would have been so nice to go to school each day and learn something that was not violent. Instead when she did send me (now and then, of course.) I sat there like the local idiot. Where was I, where were the other children? I didn't even want to open a book because I didn't know what they were talking about. I could never catch up. What was a take-away sum? I didn't know. What were additions? What was geography. I was lost forever to the school system.

I knew how to bless myself in the holy water and how to genuflect in front of the Altar of God. They loaned me a veil in which to take my first Holy Communion. It was so big I tripped over it in the aisle. I also learned how to go to confession and lie to the priest because I was afraid to tell the truth. He wanted to hear my sins so I made up some, and that was another happy man — good girl! I learned to sing hymns in Latin. So there was nothing wrong with my head in regards to learning and I could read. I was lucky in that respect.

Then there was the day when my mother took me with her to the wine bar at Central and once again she left me outside on the corner with the same instructions as always: 'Don't move.' So that's where I stood. But today was to be different. When afternoon came and she had not returned, I thought perhaps she had gone with a man and would rush up later, but no, this was not the case. She had apparently forgotten me altogether that day and had caught the train and bus home to Chullora. It was only after my father came home that day from work on the council that they realised I had been left in the city and it was getting late. My father had to make the long trip back to the city to get me. That took time because it was not a bus or train service as we know it today. It was a slow, long, time consuming trip. Meanwhile, I stood where she had left me in the morning. I didn't remember her ever doing this, so I just

25

waited. When the streetlights came on, I was still in the same spot, well trained and lucky. I say that because I was there for the taking and nobody did. As darkness fell the number of people dwindled where I was. That was good because I remember wishing I could lay down on the ground. I was so tired and I didn't want people to look at me then. They might know about me and get me into trouble with him and her. Then I heard the whistle. It was coming from the footpath under the archways of the station and I knew it was him. I guess I was glad but nervous. Because of that bloody whistle, would it be my fault she left me and my fault he had to come all this way to get me? Would he hit me for it or what? Prepare, prepare, always be ready and don't cry.

Well he stopped just before he got to me, gave a loud whistle and just beckoned me with one hand to go to him. I did, but fell over skinning my knees. I think it was because I was so tired and had stood in one spot so many hours, or something like cramp, stiffness or whatever. No tears. He never looked down and I don't think he even looked at my face. No words were spoken to me and, of course, being so tired, I fell asleep on the train. The bright lights in the train made my eyes close. He just pushed me when we got to Punchbowl Station and we got out of the train. However, it was not over yet — the rotten bus had not waited for this train and that meant a walk home.

Now was the time for my 'Hail Mary's' to work: I felt I couldn't walk so many miles. But prayers didn't work and he started to walk quickly in anger. The body language was there and so I trailed behind him in the darkness. That was the best part. It was dark and I loved the dark. Well, we did get there and she was standing at the back door. I could smell the grog and the onions. She had been doing a bit of drinking while waiting I guess. Well, if I expected to be greeted with open arms or some show of joy, I was wrong. She just said to him, thank Christ I was still there — it could have been difficult for them. Then she told me to go to bed. I was hungry, but not game to start something by asking her for something to eat, so I went to bed, glad the day was finally over for me and sleep was my reward.

You know, it was strange having a mother who you knew got rid of things she didn't like or destroyed them, because if she didn't like me — and I was sure of that — I was surely on the list of things to get rid of sooner or later.

Another punishment was to put an old ladder up against the toilet wall and make me climb up on top of the roof. The heat was unbearable up there and it was made of iron. I was afraid of falling off because she would put the ladder on the ground cutting off my exit. Sometimes she would get me down after a short time, but other times she left me a long time. One day though, she left me there too long. I got bad sunstroke and she could hardly get me down because I was so sick I could not help myself. When I was finally down, all I could do was be dizzy and vomit, rolling on the lino in the house. Thank my stars she never did it again. That's a bad sickness to have. Even now, if I am too long in the sun, I start to go through it in my mind. It makes me sick and I have to switch my thoughts off.

But as the time goes on and my mind allows me to write, again I just really want to stop and put it all back into the hole it was in, because it gets so hard to continue when you want it to stop straight away. You really don't want to work this hard at it and because it's been hard all your life and painful, you hope it will now be easy. Well, it's not, but — and that's a very big but — you are on the way like you have never been before. You are on your way through the gates of hell. The trick is to hang in there. You already have the proof that you have the guts to hang in there — after all, you're a survivor. So here I go again.

My mother had taught me how to lift the men's wallets or money purses while they were busy with her and how to take some notes out, but always leave some there for them to see. Then the money was put in her purse in separate sections, never all together in case of trouble. I was an expert at it and never got caught, nor did she. I was well trained by her; I never made mistakes and never talked so I was better than most adults. I didn't steal from her, so she had herself a good partner. I don't think any other prostitute has had such a good racket going, but no wonder they hated her. Nobody else seemed to have a kid work with them, only her, and while she carried a razor with her, who was going to tell her to stop it. Nobody, I guess, and when I think about it, I only saw my mother frightened once.

That was in Oxford Street, Sydney one afternoon as we walked back to the station on the corner of the park. We had been in the room with a very greasy, fat, smelly man. I had lifted his money, separated it and put it in mum's purse, as always, and then sat in the corner trying not to look big. I crouched on the floor as she told me if the men didn't want to use me, I had to look small and quiet, so I did this, as ordered. When they were finished he and my mother had a short, but violent argument during which he put a piece of paper in front of my mother's face. She didn't even lift a hand and this, believe me, was unusual. Nobody ever won arguments with her or pushed or bullied her, only my father. But this fat man did and she got nothing off him except the money I lifted. I think she liked me for a moment at least.

But that was not the end of it. As we walked to the station two men in suits and hats stepped out from nowhere and jammed her in. I thought it was just men she had sex with.

It seemed to have a strange affect on her. They did not raise their voices, but whatever it was, she looked scared. One of the men patted my head and told her I was a nice big girl. Now he never even looked at me when he said it, but looked at her and by now my mother was white with fear. I do not know to this day who or what they were, but it was bad. She was in some big trouble, I sensed and she couldn't hide it. Then they left and as quietly as they stepped out, they were gone. People were looking at my mother. She was acting strangely and then for the first time ever in public, she hit me across the face and yelled, "see what you did, you naughty girl. Wait till I get you home."

She dragged me by the arm to the station. People looked, but that's all. On the train I felt safe because even though I didn't know what time it was, I knew we would get home before Dad or the boys, but it would be too late for her to do anything to me then. So I had a reprieve for a time, although I knew it would come in one form or another and it would be bad. And it was. The next morning she locked me in the closet and didn't let me out until just before my brothers came home. At least that was all she did that day, so it wasn't my worst day.

Our next trip to town was not to be forgotten by me. It was to haunt me forever. My mother met the man at Mark Foys where lots of her friends from East Sydney met their men, or customers, whatever you want to call them. It was a busy corner back in those days. I liked the look of that big store and all the steps. The ladies all dressed up like my mother wearing cute hats, fur collars, but I don't suppose they were all doing what my mother was doing. Anyway, back to that day. It was different, I felt it and the strange thing is that many times in life I will get a feeling that something is about to happen. It does and maybe it was because I was always waiting for something to happen in one way or another. So off we went up Oxford Street and then we were back in that street again and I felt worse than usual. My mother, me and the man were there, and it started off strangely. She didn't want me in the room with them. Maybe he didn't want anything from me. I stood and sat on the arm of a fat lounge in the corner. "Always take a small space, she said and don't talk." That was OK by me. I had nothing to say anymore anyway.

The big fat redhead lady in the flower satin coat just looked at me and went on eating. Then she went to answer the door and came back with the prettiest lady I had ever seen, with white skin, pink cheeks, big eyes, looking like a doll in a black dress. The redhead called out to my mother, "Jess come here now. It's Liz to see you."

In what seemed like a second, my mother was in the room

with not a single stitch of clothing on and holding that cork in her hand. I saw it straight away and knew it meant trouble. Liz said something to Mum and she screamed "You bastard!" and in a flash the blade in the cork got poor Liz in the face and neck. She was screaming, holding her face. Blood was like a hose rushing out between her fingers. Oh where was the Guardian Angel? Now my heart was beating with the screams. There was blood everywhere and then the redhead pushed Liz out yelling, 'Run you bitch, run.'

My mother was covered in blood. The redhead made her hurry to get clean and dressed, saying 'Get out quick with the kid.' I looked down — I was crouching in the corner — and could see there was blood on one of my socks. Oh gosh, she might kill me for that. She was so mad today.

Then the redhead saw blood on her fish and chips on the table and started swearing. She threw it in a piece of newspaper, then went and got a dish and something to clean the place up with.

Where was my mother? I wanted to go. Then she came back into the room clean and dressed like nothing was wrong. The redhead was angry and said something. Then we left without the man. I didn't know where he'd got to.

Out in the street it was still hot and we walked down Oxford Street as if nothing had happened. I kept looking for poor Liz and couldn't stop looking back. My mother wrenched me by the hand and bent my wrist so that I couldn't do anything but walk fast beside her. We caught the train in the tunnel near Mark Foys — no walking back to Central today. She had not spoken to me, as was the custom. She only spoke to me if somebody on the train ever spoke. I was swinging my legs looking out the window when I remembered the blood on my sock. I stopped swinging and looked at it. The stain was about the size of a three pence. My mother saw it then and all she said was 'Your nose been bleeding again?' That was that. She had already switched off, but I couldn't switch off. My insides were twitching. Why did it happen? Was Liz alone like me? I suppose so.

Who wants to be part of a horror story; who wants to believe that there are people who get their pleasure from hurting others and getting away with it? They have power. I must now unlearn everything my family taught me, or I thought I could, but it didn't work that way.

Even though I am old now and more aware of what was taking place in the days of my childhood, it is still horrific to think about and, of course, I know razor gangs were causing people to think twice before doing the wrong thing to each other. Of course my mother used it to keep control and to punish the enemy. It was the best protection you could have. More so if you were good with it and my mother sure was. She mixed with strong people, so she needed strong actions to save herself. The area she came from taught her well, so, of course, my mother did not turn into a bad woman overnight!

In those days there were many gangs in the vice scene. Violence went with the territory. Thugs used razors; prostitutes used razors because a razor was better than a gun. Guns killed and you could spend a lot of time in jail for murder, but rarely did you kill with the razor and nobody forgets it if it happens to them. After all the scars are terrible, the pain is terrible and each day for the rest of your life you will see it and be reminded of who and why.

The razor in the cork was made by my father for her to use. She used it well. I remember blood, always blood. Why did no-one ever send her to jail? How many faces did she ruin? I sometimes think about Liz. Did she live? Did she marry with that poor face? Maybe she did and maybe she had a child and told it what happened to her. Maybe her child will read my book. I am sorry for what my mother did with that rotten cork razor. Why did it happen, and if only I could have stopped it.

It was hard to block out, but I learned long ago to deal with frightening and unsavoury truths by simply blocking them out, so that the pattern of abuse became a way of life.

To the unknowing, a question that could be asked is how

could a person endure unheard of torture and sexual torment as a child, and live such an outwardly ordinary existence? The fact is that the torture, carried out by my mother, seemed to pale next to the hurt of rejection and the feeling of being unloved. The feeling when I was young was of total loneliness; it was a life without any demonstration of affection that was not of a perverted nature. The emptiness of living without sense of any future love; no child pampering; no sense of worth. Each day drifted into the next. The train rides into the city were the only relief from the before and the after scenes of my life hat mostly led me into another form of hell.

My mother never really tried to hide her dislike of me. Later on in my life many people remarked to me about the derogatory way she spoke of me, despite my accomplishments. My brothers had wooden beds with mattresses and went to school compared to my erratic school and chaff beds. I had also noticed that her dislike of my brothers was a closely guarded secret until later in her life when she confessed to me of the way she really felt about them. It was quite a surprise, I can tell you. I do not know whether any other members of the family were also abused by my parents, but if they were then it would explain a lot of things.

As it is I have still enough memories and pain to fill another book on abuse from people other than my mother and father. If I lived in America I would not be silenced by laws that forbid me to write about certain people who also sexually, mentally and physically abused me. But I am silenced here. You may remember, as I explained earlier, my father would hit me on the head, so as to leave no visible marks. When he did this, almost every time my nose would spurt blood, and this would continue over many days on and off until it stopped itself and, perhaps, healed a little. Then without warning, it would spurt again, no matter where I was or what I was doing. This terrible affliction lasted until late in my thirties. I always pretended it was nothing, but it caused me to feel horror and get flashbacks of my childhood filled with fear, just as if my father was hitting me then.

When my now dear second husband was courting me, it happened so often and with such force that he took me to doctor after doctor for help. Mostly that just resulted in packing my nose and receiving some kind words from them, although I remember one doctor from Campsie questioning me about my past life and injuries. Of course, I said nothing, but lived in fear of it happening. It was a terrible reminder of my father and the threats from my mother that if I talked, she would tell people I was mad like Uncle Willey (who never existed), plus the repeated threat that I would go to the place for mad people, locked in a room with blood on the floor. So even at that age the bleeding made me relive it all. It was horrible and my fear of blood was very strong and still is today. However, it has not occurred to me for many years since I was married and that has been wonderful for me.

As I look back I can see how cruel it was that, on the rare occasions when I was sent to school, the other children made fun of the way I walked. No adult was ever curious or interested enough to want to know why a little girl walked in a way that suggested she had something wrong between her legs — or were Catholic nuns not allowed to discuss earthly things, and did other people all wear blinkers to protect themselves?

I remember being on a bus with other children, and my humiliation when word went down the bus that I must have soiled myself as I could not keep my legs together because of pain. The children were a little afraid at school to be so loud and rude in front of the God-like nuns, but on the bus it was their own territory, and how I wished that someone would protect me then. It was more punishment for something I had not done myself. Life seemed to be made up of pain — when was it going to end!

When I walked the rest of the way home from the bus stop, my poor young mind was confused. I wanted to go in the house and say: 'Mum, I'm hurting. Please fix me up and make it better.' But how do you ask the monster who had hurt you to make it better? After all, so many times she had told me it was my fault that I got hurt and that if I had done everything the way she told me, it would not have happened; it was my own fault. Always my fault!

Sometimes I knew it was not my fault, such as the time when she had gone to the city without me and my brothers had control. They took me with them to the bread factory, Gartrell White, down on Punchbowl Road because occasionally the baker would let kids pick up any rolls they'd dropped on the ground. The councilmen were there as well. They were putting tar on the road outside the factory and had a big drum with warm tar standing nearby.

My brothers just lifted me up and submerged my arm in it up to the shoulder. I was screaming this time because it was terrible. The workmen saw what happened and yelled out chasing my brothers away. They were running away dragging me along the ground. The workmen soon stopped chasing. I guess they felt they had done enough and had to go back to work. By the time we got home the tar had cooled and hardened on my arm or at least 80 per cent of it had, so they panicked and scraped it off with knives. My arm was burned and part skinned and I waited to see what might happen to them. Maybe something to justify my pain and shock, but nothing was said; nothing was done. They would have been in more trouble if they had kicked the dog. My arm healed in time, but the smell of tar when it's hot makes me sick today.

I guess I got fed up with it sometimes. I thought I had the answer by running away. It always seemed the right thing to do and I did.

But always the police found me and brought me back to a police station, where I'd wait for parents. One time in the night I ran away and after walking all night pushing a one-wheel barrow (with a little difficulty,) with my school uniform I realized I was not alone in this expedition. A little girl who I met as I passed her house near the shop, wanted to come with even though she didn't know me well, and she lived in a loving family, with never a mark on her. In the dark we pushed the barrow along the highway with one broken wheel and we reached Liverpool at lunchtime the next day. For those who remember Liverpool Road, it did not have the traffic of today, thank goodness. My little friend had a book of raffle tickets she brought along with her and we tried to raffle something that we didn't have. A couple of kind people bought them and we brought a tin of peas, we broke it open with a rock. Whilst sitting under a tree eating our proceeds, up came the law. They seemed to be happy to find me and took me back to Liverpool Police Station where we were queens, for a time eating their sandwiches and drinking real milk. My friend's parents collected her and I never saw her again.

The police were wonderful to me, but a little surprised when I told them where I came from. They said that no one had lost a little girl to their knowledge, so I was there for quite sometime before my father arrived. He did not look like a father whose little girl had been found alive and well. One of the policemen said so to him in no uncertain words. He asked my father what was the problem for me to run away like I did. My father was ready with the right words, 'Just a naughty girl frightening her poor dad and mum.' He said he was so worried that he couldn't smile, but he was grateful to the police for finding me. However, the policeman seemed not too happy himself with that and asked my father why he hadn't told the police in his area (Bankstown). My father said he was too busy searching the scrub near us and thought that one of his sons had done so. He was sorry and said he just wanted to take me home to my poor, worried mum. When I got home, and after the belting, he told me next time I did it, he would kill me.

Of course, it was to happen again and the next memorable runaway was to Como. I travelled alone on a train and had arrived in the night at the terminal of the railway station and walked into the bush. It was freezing and I slept in a hole with leaves over me. It was my undoing. I had almost nothing to eat and in the night something was there in the hole with me. It was a rat and it sure bit me on the calf of my right leg. I was in trouble now for sure. The next day my leg was yucky. The bite looked nasty and it was throbbing like crazy. My childish mind thought that if I got out of the bush, someone would give me something for my leg. They did — a nice big policeman. He took me to the police station and once more the law got a shock. No children reported missing, no alarm bells ringing.

This time after finding out that it was not the first time, they made him and her explain what was wrong at home. They both said there was nothing, but thought I had a mental problem. The policeman said I was brighter than any kid he'd met at my age and he warned them that if he became aware of it happening again he would look in to it further.

On the way back home they both looked scared, but sure of themselves because I had not talked and that let them know I was still living in my own silent pain of the abused child. As punishment, my mother did not treat the rat bite and I nearly lost my leg. She told me that God punished me for running away and the next time he would make me lose both legs. I believed it and never ran away again.

I knew then that God really didn't like me. He always found ways to make sure I hurt. She said he did it. So it was true, it had to be. I believed everything she said and as you may have noticed by now, I had always run away in the night, but if you ask a child what they are afraid of, it is mostly the dark. Yet I felt safer out in the dark than with my family.

This is another indication that things were very wrong in the home. I am sure people will be more alert now if, and when, this type of abuse is present. They weren't back then, unfortunately.

If it were possible to raise the dead and kill them, I would. I have confronted four other abusers still living and cleared the pain into its right order. Now even though it was by letter — with the aid of a solicitor — they know that I have survived their sexual, mental and physical abuse. I am no longer a victim. They are the criminals, the abusers. I was their victim.

Victims need help, not criticism. They need to not live in fear of a touch, but feel the simple and honest hands of someone who will know about their pain; someone who has been down the same road, though not necessarily of abuse.

I will dedicate the remainder of my life to victims, so that there will be an understanding of pain which can't let go till we let go.

My half-brother Bob never sexually abused me, as a child. In fact, when he came to visit it was to have intercourse with our mother. He always went mad at her for my neglected hair and appearance. He would tell her to at least comb my hair. When she ignored this appeal he would comb my curls and try to show her how, but sick sex was the main issue of the visit.

They made no attempt to conceal the fact from me and had intercourse as I watched. On the same visits he would bring a gift for me. It was a double-edged sword. He pretended everything was fine, cleaned me up and gave me a present, screwed my mother (his mother also) and left. When I got older he would describe mum as a lush. I did not know what it meant at the time, but I heard him correctly many times say "you know, Mary, mother's problem is she is a lush." It wasn't till many years later that I found out what a lush was.

As you can see, this was not sexual abuse of me, but at the same time it was a form of abuse as he indulged in sexual activities in front of me, and he was guilty of failing to protect a child. Therefore it was a form of abuse.

Ralph nicknamed Goody, my eldest brother living at home had me frightened for as long as I can remember. It's my opinion that when he looked at me, it was with a cold and cruel detachment, without one ounce of compassion. His sexual acts with me were as if he wanted to see me demoralised. He showed no pleasure, nor displeasure, but just complete dominance. He wanted the sex act and I was there for him. His love of cruelty towards me never ended, but just grew. To this day when I think of him and what it was like, I wish to vomit. My other two abusers were twins Ben, and Bill who was by far more calculating. His sexual abuse of me was because he was the boss of the two of them. He was as cruel to animals as he was to me and showed the others that his way, and his way only, was how to do things whether it was sexual with me, or mental cruelty to me. The other one was weak, easily led and did things to please the others. He did many cruel things and always as if he had to. I don't mean that he was forced, but that he wanted to show the bullies he was one as well.

When I confronted them through Victims of Crime, they no longer held power over me. I will never forgive them, but I no longer have fear of them, and today they would never get away with mental, sexual or physical abuse of me. I do know that there was no kindness towards me from any of them, and now I feel that they must not expect kindness from me, just the truth.

At about this time my father and mother were discussing some sort of trouble she was in. I don't really know what it was about. In fact, I could be wrong as to the time it happened, so I can't put the year to it, but whatever year it was, it was not very good for them. They were trying to get away from something. They nailed up the house and I waxed cloth with my father to make it waterproof. He made a caravan from the wagon we had and covered it with the waxed cloth to keep the rain out. We had a couple of horses which my parents decided to use to take the caravan and us, together with a sulky on a long and sickening trip to Yenda to pick fruit and live off the land, using me to beg for food on behalf of the family at country properties and stations. It worked because I was a little girl and must have looked like a wretched little thing. They gave willingly. I mean they gave food, sometimes bread or eggs of left over mutton bones it helped.

During the course of this trip we camped at Yass. One day when we were alongside the river an Aboriginal man approached my mother in a threatening manner. She quickly picked up an axe, pushing me behind her and told him off and he fled. My mother said, "their not getting you, like they tried to get me." The man spent the next three days watching the camp from a distance, standing on one leg. He wouldn't go back to his camp, maybe because he was shamed for being chased off by a woman.

During our time at Yass my mother took me to the Catholic convent and asked them to take me for a couple of weeks. Each day I went and was the butt of ridicule. It always started with prayer and then they would say 'Aren't we lucky to have poor little Mary with us for a short visit. This dear little girl lives on the road with horses and caravans. She's our own little gypsy,' then the pat on the head. All the other kids looked at me in my rags and made sure I sat alone. The children told their parents about the little gypsy girl and their parents warned "don't talk to gypsies".

The only good thing was that the nuns made tomato sandwiches cut into little triangles. I had never seen before the delicate way they were done. Also the sandwiches were placed on a plate with flowers on it and a glass of milk. I could get to like this very much and started to wish I could stay there, but that was not to be.

My mother spoke to the nuns telling them it was time to move on because of the trouble with the Aboriginal man trying to take me. The nuns asked my mother and father to leave me with them and promised to give me a good life. Of course, my parents refused, my mother saying "I was worth more to her on the road." I knew they would not let me be too long with anybody in case I talked, so we moved on day after day until we reached Yenda.

It was many years later that my second husband Eberhard and I visited the convent. We spoke to some lovely nuns and I discussed the time I had spent their as a child. They introduced me to a very elderly nun who was at the convent during the time I was there, she was very little and frail. I wondered if she did remember the little gypsy girl! The elderly nun said, "I can't say for sure that I remember you, but I can say for sure that I remember a little girl who didn't know what to do with a triangle sandwiches."

CHAPTER FOUR

It was fair punishment that my father would die in Yass in a car smash in the year of 1966. Maybe it was a payback. (Maybe there was some justice after all.)

I remember having to identify my father's body at the morgue behind the little hospital in sight of the convent where I had been. The police asked my four brothers one by one if they would identify the body. They all refused. The police were shocked when it came to me to do it, the youngest and a girl to identify him.

I was then left to face the bogey man — he who took away my childhood and represented pain, filth and depravity. I had to look at him, but the police at Yass were the kindest and most caring people anyone could meet. The head policeman chose another one of the kindly policeman to go with me. We went up the little hill by car and through the little hospital hallway out the back, through the paspalum to a little tiny shed. He went in and pulled out the tray, then came and gently took my hand. As if he knew my sad story. He led me to the tray and told me to take a deep breath. Holding tightly to his hand, I looked at the face of the Devil. It was my father, he was dead. The identification was complete. He had returned to Hell.

'But now I must take you back to the trip or I will mix you up, so that you won't be able to follow the story. While travelling those hot, dusty roads to Yenda, I did come into contact again with kindness. We met a nice kind man who felt sorry for me and gave me a little whippet dog, a dear little live present and all mine. I really liked that puppy. After we finally arrived in Yenda, my mother had returned by train to Sydney, leaving us all camped by the side of the irrigation system.

The morning after she left my brothers called me to come and look at something in the water. The water was in a channel type system with cement sides sloping down into the water that to me always looked dark and forbidding. Today was no exception, but it was worse.

They, my brothers, the three of them, had prepared another horror for me. They had thrown my little puppy in and, of course, he was frantically trying to scratch his way out of the water up the cement walls, but it was useless. They laughingly pushed each other with joy and made me watch my dog drown. They copied my words of fright and fear saying I would be next.

I still see that horror in my head to this day, and how many times do I wish that I had not decided to go into the depth of such pain? At least twice a day. Sometimes I am full of courage and know the feeling that it is good to put it on paper to let others share the pain. Then bang, it starts to hurt so much that being back in the cupboard was easier than this.

Maybe this will change with exposure — pain out, no pain in. I wish somebody could tell me something —why did Catholics give out those holy pictures of an angel hovering over two little children to save them from falling through a rickety old broken walkway? There was no angel hovering over me to save me. I remember the nuns at the schools at Punchbowl and Yass telling me how lucky I was to have a name such as Mary and to be one of God's special children. They said I was so lucky, I could become a novice in the convent. But what was lucky about my life? They told me it was a good life I had, but hell they refused to look and see that there was only pain and isolation.

Wow! What confusion they shot through me. If this was a good life, what was a bad one like? I did not commence school until I was over seven years old and from then on it was a place she sent me to when she did not need me. That was not very often as her sick needs came before everything else. She placed herself above everyone and everything and to go against her was to go against the Devil. I was not the only one to believe she was the Devil. She left her mark on a lot of people.

I remember how she was always insulting people with her vile language and obscenities. She did so to a neighbour opposite us, a widow with two sons, one of whom was pianist. My mother hated all women so she made them target for insults, until one day when she had been to this poor lady, the woman called the police. A court case followed where my mother told her off but she lost when my father did not answer the court's question in the way my mother wanted. She was given a warning.

In court she had said my father witnessed the conversation between herself and the lady opposite and that she had not said the terrible things that the woman claimed she had, despite witnesses saying it was true. She really was guilty. My father's denial was the biggest mistake of his life. But that is later in my story.

I remember another amazing thing about my mother. That was her ability to believe that only she could win and she did! Later in her old age after my father's death, she won a court battle against another man with whom she had been carrying on, even though he was supposed to be happily married. She soon had him doing what she wanted, including odd jobs around her house. I caught them in bed once when I went to take her shopping to her. I told her that what she was doing was very wrong as he had a wife. She called me a nun and told me to come back when I left the convent. But I think the man felt bad and in a matter of days he wiped her off. So she took him to court for some bad work or something and won, of course. Then she said to me 'That's called a pay back' and laughed. She was in her late sixties then, but she was still the same person. Rotten and hell bent on revenge against anyone who stood up to her.

Even people who hardly knew her could not forget her. Many

times I have seen women who look like my mother. The feeling is incredible. My first reaction is fright; the second is to run and the third is, why didn't she love me? If she had only loved me, what a daughter I would have been.

I looked after her in her old age with tenderness and respect that she did not deserve or earn. I'd had enough cruelty in my life and had no wish to be the same as her. I guess right up till she died, I was wishing she would tell me that she loved me, even if she never said she was sorry. Such a shame, but it never took place. She had plenty of time, but apparently couldn't.

Not all women who have babies are mothers. I hope my children never think of me like that because even though I must have made a million mistakes, not loving them was not amongst them, for in my heart, to be loved is the most important thing that a child can have, because the memory lives on long after and into old age. Of course, back then I just wanted to be loved like the other children I had seen at school and like the girls who went to dancing classes.

However, there is another twist to this story. Even though I had never been disobedient, I was always good at being whatever they wanted. So when I went to school one day, I decided to do what I wanted for a change. There were some girls in the same class as me who went to dancing lessons at the Osborne Dance School run by a talented family consisting of the mother and two daughters. Their school was based on talent and integrity. It was a proud moment for any child enrolled in that fine school. That was what I wanted also. It did not daunt me that I'd never be allowed to go, so I asked her. Not only did she say no, but I got a hiding for asking. I didn't go to school for a while after that.

The funny part of the story is that I had seen the little uniform that the children wore at the dance class, and had stolen a pillowcase from the clothesline which was off my mother's bed. I cut the sides and the end. I put my poor little arms and head through the openings and was ready, I thought, for dancing class. I planned to go after school the very next time I was there. It was not even a nice white pillowcase like the colour of their uniforms. It was more greyish, as I remember.

So my chance came. I had hidden it out the front in the grass. Off to school I went and it didn't matter anymore that I was different to the other kids. I was going to be a dancer. I had a tunic uniform just like the others, I thought, and sure enough after school off I went, into the hall where the mothers were sitting around the room against the wall dressing their little girls in snow white tunics. What a sight I must have looked. I took the school tunic off and with my oversized bloomers belonging to my mother dropping down my legs, I pulled them up and rolled the top over, put my pillowcase on and walked over into one of the rows of little girls. All the dancers were looking at me, but it didn't matter.

For the first time in my life I was happy, I was going to dance. It didn't matter that they had taps on their shoes and I didn't. In fact, nothing mattered at that moment. The poor dance teachers, what did they think? But they were real angels and they let me heel toe, heel toe, tap tap. The piano was playing, no one stopped me, and I can understand why. Who would have the heart to stop this poor little girl having a few moments of joy? Even the way I looked must have drawn sympathy from these wonderful ladies. I did not realise that you paid for dance lessons.

Well, I did this for two classes and then the third time, just as I was believing that even the closet was a dream, the bubble burst! 'A nice note to take to your mummy,' the lovely lady said, I got home late from school, so it all happened on the same day. My mother was waiting when I arrived home note in hand, dancing pillowcase in my bag. It was never to be forgotten. She hit first, knocking me over on the ground. She grabbed my hair, dragging me behind her still on the ground. Then she said that this would be the last time I would come home late. Then she saw the note in my hand, grabbed it, read it and made me chew it, eat it and swallow it. If I didn't she said she would get water and wash it down. I remembered the water, so I chewed, sucked and swallowed the note. She then opened my bag and there was her pillowcase. Gosh, where was God?

He should have been there then. Finally she saw where I had cut the arms and neck out of it. This was it! She stopped, sent me inside and said very quietly, 'tomorrow, Jew bastard, tomorrow.'

Well, tomorrow did come and no school, so I knew it was going to be my day again and it was. She filled the bath halfway up with cold water and I was made to sit in it from morning till afternoon. It was one of the most terrible experiences you could be put through. My bottom was sticking to the bath, numb and stinging at the same time. I went from freezing cold to boiling hot. My face was on fire and I wanted to lay down and sleep. I got hungry, but then I wasn't anymore. Just tired and my back was on fire. I put my hands on the side of the bath and rested my head on them. Of course, she spotted me and made me sit up straight. For the first time in my young life I prayed – not the way people in church do, but I said all the things I had picked up at school.

That was the end of that dance class and any other dance class — or for that matter, anything that had a normal look to it. It was pretty awful to have to live like this, but thank goodness I can see some other sides to things. It even got close to funny now in my mind.

Things had been pretty bad at home. My mother was angry with some man and that always spelt trouble for me, so I had been locked in the wardrobe nearly all day. I was sick from heat and fear and my mouth was sore so when night came and I was allowed to sleep, it was great.

The next day she wrote a note, never telling me what she had written, and packed me off to school (St Therese, Lakemba, by this time). When I got there it was late. All the kids were in by this time and a sister was just walking down from the convent. She caught me in the school playground, note in hand, and asked me why I was in school at that moment. I told her I had walked. Even the worldly, Godly lady knew that was a long way. She read the note and said your poor mummy is sick, eh Mary? I said yes; after all the nun wanted this answer. But oh hell, she said 'You go home, Mary, and look after your dear mummy till she is better.' Back to the hellhole I went. Shit, where was that guardian angel now? Fancy sending me back when I had just got out!

Next time you think the odds are stacked against you, think of this story. I realise now that I missed out on a lot of things and one of these was a grandmother. All the time I must have had a darling grandmother because I remember when she sent letters and a beautiful scarf just for me. She had said it was for the little girl, so my mother promptly burned the scarf and the letters saying that the Pommy bitch overlooked her for me. She never let me talk about it, so I didn't.

Since their deaths I have many times been in contact with my father's family. They even sent me photos and a scarf to make up for the one my mother burned. My father's sisters are real darlings and I will never tell them anything sad about my father. My grandmother was a very lovely and gracious lady. I am glad she has passed and doesn't know about the monster who was her son.

My paternal grandmother

These people destroyed my character. My family took away my right to have aunts and uncles for my children. They took away my right to have nephews and nieces, to have a family to look up to and with whom to feel safe and protected. I don't need that now, but I should have at least had the chance to be a loved little girl, not a sexual partner on which to practice. I just wanted to play with dolls and be loved.

Little babies are not born bad nor are they born with sins. Someone older and perverted has to make them believe they are with fear and intimidation.

One cold winter morning my mother was quieter than normal and I waited for her to warm up and start on me again, but it was not to be this day. When I look back now, it's easy to see why. She was in labour and it was not the first time I had seen this type of behaviour with her. I had seen it at least two or three times before, but not quite like this day. She was moaning and had a big copper full of water boiling away. There was smoke from the wood and steam right through the house. It was strange because she kept putting the boiling water from the copper into the bathtub and then putting cold water into it until it was enough to reach half way. Then she put a big dish next to the bath and for a little while I thought it was for me, but found out later that it was not. She then told me to stand next to the tub and not move away. She got in and after sometime the water turned red. Then I saw the doll — or at least that was what I thought it was. After a few minutes she put it in the dish next to the bath and I played with it till she got out, dried herself and rinsed the bath.

That was that — she had aborted a baby and let me play with it thinking it was a doll. After she cleaned the bath again, she tipped the water down the drain and burned the baby in the copper fire. She then lay down till my father and brothers came home. Not a word was said by her, but stranger than that not a word by me.

That was my life. Until the next time I saw an aborted baby — it was mine. I remember the fight. She blamed my father and my father blamed her. She said it was his and he said it was one of her men friends, but I knew and I refused to say whose it was except that it was not one of her men friends. She fixed me with a soap pencil and so it was over in no time at all, or at least that's what she said and who was I to argue with that woman! The memory of it will be with me forever, the pain, the blood, the disgust I felt for myself.

Why didn't I die then? I was about 12 or 13. I am not sure. My life has been like a massive bushfire that has swept through me, causing pain and destruction in every part of my mind and body. Now, as I sift through the ashes, I am finding pieces of life from the past that even though they are scarred, they can live again. Maybe not as they were originally meant to be, but in a way that will allow me to grow from that tortured child into an understanding and powerful ally of the abused and, perhaps to, use my knowledge far greater than those who know no pain.

I am very shaken and affected by what I have written because, as all victims know, just looking at the abuse is one thing, then talking about it is another. But to read about it on paper is the realisation that you really lived through it the only way you knew how and you can call it anything you like — I call it survival!

Now, for the moment, enough of how I feel and let me put you back into the story of my life and how my parents ticked.

In my day there was a case called 'The Pyjama Girl Mystery'. The police had the body of a young woman whom nobody came forward to identify or claim. So they kept her in a bath of very formaldehyde to preserve her, allowing certain people to look at her to see if she belonged to them. My mother was very upset about the case and told my father that she believed it was her sister, Mary — the one I was named after — and that she thought Mary had been killed. So even though she didn't like anything to do with the police, she did go and view the body. She said it was not her sister, but her sister was never heard of again. Back then who knows what happened to her!

Anyway, my mother's obsession about 'The Pyjama Girl' case was really understandable as my mother had originally spent some of her life in Victoria and the body of the girl was found in a culvert near Albury, which really was closer to Victoria than Sydney.

She was also about 26 years old, just like my mother's sister. She also had a plump face, bobbed hair, gold inlays in her teeth. All these things fitted and were the same description as my mother's sister. My mother talked with my father about some trouble she herself was in over the border, the reason why they had to move, and that combined with her associations in the city in Sydney, made her feel really sure it was a payback. She told him she expected something like that to happen because she said money was tight and you have to be quick or dead. She talked about undercutting prices and giving them what they wanted, but keeping control. She sure did.

She was always telling him that he was too weak with other men; his strength was only his tool and you can't knock a bloke out with that, she said.

Now, unfortunately for me, I do remember the day the man came whom she killed. He arrived early in the morning. Men didn't usually come early to our place. Maybe it was because of the distance from town or, perhaps, something else.

Most of the men sold matches, watches and laces— anything I guess to make money, but once they talked to my mother, their money-making was forgotten. I don't really know if she ever got any money off these flim-flam men or just their company and sex, of course. It was her game.

This particular day the man had a suit on, but did not carry any case or bag and that let me know he wasn't selling. She was more than a little sharp with him, so I knew also that one of us was in for a bad time. It started with me. She put me in the dog pen and went back inside. For a long time I could hear her arguing with the man and then they stopped. Lots of time went by and to my surprise, she came out and got me from the pen. The man was laughing. He told her she was a smart woman to keep the dog on a chain and put the kid in the pen. He really enjoyed the joke.

I noticed there was a flask on the table that he must have had on him when he arrived. It was not hers, I knew that. They were both taking sips from the flask. She then suggested he should have some fun with me, but he said he was not into babies and certainly not interested in dirty games with me. I guess that surprised her and made her look a bit bad.

He told her she should stop it because it was big copper trouble. She asked him if he thought he was a fuckin' saint or something. It was then they started to argue again and he gave her a slap across the head. She screamed at him and said, 'Don't think you gonna get away with that, you know.' He just laughed at her. I could have told him she meant what she said, but he looked like he wasn't afraid of anyone. He would find out anyway. I didn't like this man, but he had gone mad on her and that was good. Not many people did that, but boy, he was going to pay.

Then I heard that whistle out the front. She and I knew it was my father and she said something to the man. He grabbed the flask and put it in his pocket. My father walked in and my mother made a big fuss about kissing him as if he was something special. He smelt the grog and had the shits straight away, but nevertheless he shook the man's hand when she introduced him. My father talked to him and they started laughing as if they were friends. A little later my father got his tobacco tin and opened it. He took some money out and gave it to the man, telling him to get a bottle or two. The man kept saying it was too far to walk for a drink, but my father was persistent and kept telling him he would be back well before dark. He said he would make up a swag for him, give him a lamp and food and then pick him a good spot out in the scrub, but close to the house.

When my father said the other kids were too big and might talk if they saw him, the man finally agreed and father walked with him outback into the scrub. He was alone when he came back and as soon as he walked in, he cuffed me over the head and told me to put my big nose to sleep. I knew what he meant. He didn't have to hit me or tell me. Silence was the name of the game.

The next day, as soon as the boys had gone to school, my father went out the back into the scrub. On returning he was carrying the swag and lamp. The man was with him and looked awful as if he had slept in his suit that was all crumpled and messy. He told my mother to get him a cup of coffee and chicory which she did. Then he said he wanted a bath, but my father said that could wait awhile. My mother said she would put me in the bedroom so that they could talk, but the man asked why as they had talked in front of me yesterday, so she just shoved me into the corner. They then opened a bottle of plonk and started drinking. Soon it got a bit loud and they were arguing about some money. Eventually the man told my father he was getting out. He stood up. He was standing in front of the stove. My mother screamed something at him and raised her hand as if to slap his face. He moved his head to one side and because she was smaller than him, she caught him in the side of the throat. It was terrible.

She had that rotten blade in her hand again, but this time it was not a scar on his face that she gave him. She had sliced his throat open. Blood gushed out, but he didn't scream. He just made a horrible gurgling sound and was spitting blood and pumping it out at the same time. Then my father hit her away with the back of his hand. She kept yelling things at the man, but he was down on the lino by now and my father yelled at her to shut up, saying "You've done him in, you stupid razor happy bastard."

Then she suddenly spotted me in the corner. How I wished I wasn't there. I felt for sure she was going to do the same to me because she still had that blade in her hand, blood dripping off it. I was so scared then, I actually wet my pants and for this I knew she could kill me because I did it without her telling me to do it, but she never said a word. She just grabbed my hand, took me into the bedroom and put me in the wardrobe. I was shaking all over and didn't know how to stop. I was really afraid — what was happening to the man and what was going to happen to me today. This was different and now it was quiet in the wardrobe and I couldn't hear anything. Maybe they had run away and left me locked in. Then I heard her voice. She said; "wait till I get the whitening off me."

A little later she came back and let me out of the hell hole. I don't know if I was glad or sad because I didn't want to see the man and the blood again. What about me now, was it my turn? Or was it better in the wardrobe? Either way, I would be in trouble. But strangely enough, I thought, as I went into the other room there was no sign of the man; there was no blood. Where did it all go? The walls around the stove were all fresh white-washed. There was no man on the lino and no blood on it. There was just a funny smell and even today I can smell it sometimes. It's terrible when I have these flashbacks. Thank the stars it's in black and white. But the sounds and smells are in the air and in my mind forever. I really do wish I could pretend it didn't happen. It would be so much easier.

Now I must try to explain what I think they did with the man's body. I remember what I saw, but don't know if it confirms that it was him. I never saw the man again, but the next morning my father was in the bathroom and I could hear sawing, chopping and a whole lot of noise. They started to hurry before the boys came in after school. They had not stopped to eat or drink, nor did I. I remember seeing little piles wrapped in hessian and him putting them in the kero tins under the house and him making sure the dog was on the chain.

When they had this stuff hidden they cleaned up and washed the bathroom and themselves. Then they started preparing food on the stove for tea. My father kept looking at me with a look I knew well. It was a threat in itself. My silence was assured, but my father and mother still had a problem.

The following day I went into the bathroom to look at what my father might have been doing in there yesterday. I wanted to find the man, I think, even though I guess I knew he was in pieces under the house.

When you are young fear can turn to curiosity and children want to look no matter how bad things are. But, of course, he wasn't there and the bath was clean. However, under one of the legs of the bath there was a finger. I didn't touch it, but went to my father and said cunningly that there was something in the bathroom. He rushed in and I pointed to it. I knew I had to pretend that I didn't know what it was. He pushed me out and then came out, walked to the dog and threw it at him. The dog wasn't really interested.

At that moment my father told my mother to get me out of the way, so she put me in the wardrobe again. I don't know why because I had already seen it all, so what was there to hide? It was a long time before she let me out. When she did I was given some food and allowed to sit on the floor, but away from where they were eating. I could hear them talking. He said something about Milperra River; that we could cook prawns and stay overnight. My mother said it was a good idea.

I felt excited that we were going somewhere to cook and maybe have fun. What happened next was right under my brothers' noses. He took what I am sure was the man's body all chopped and wrapped up to Milperra and while we were doing things such as lighting the fire and setting up camp, he put the packages in the river. Up and down he went and washed the kero tins in the river because they stank. I could smell them all the way there. My brothers said nothing. To make it worse my father cooked the prawns that were caught in the same tins — and everyone of us ate them. The thought sure makes me sick now, but it happened that way and that's all there is to it.

CHAPTER FIVE

Each time in my life when an argument, fight or any form of violence started, I was sick with fear because it usually meant that I would pay in one way or another and mostly end up being the loser. Even now to this day I hate violence of any form in movies, books, television and even in the news. It is only a reminder of when I was with them. So I avoid violence on or off the screen.

Now I must tell you that until the day I wrote of my mother and father and the man in the suit whose throat she cut, I had always felt so very upset and hesitant about the telling of this terrible event. For days and days I wondered how I could tell the truth. My counsellor told me I would write it if and when my mind was ready, not before. So I started to write of other things that had taken place and not to force myself into a frightening situation. I felt better and then I started writing about that horrific day. I felt all right, so I wrote for at least four hours, each thing as I saw it and after I had finished I was drained, but OK, perfectly in control, satisfied that I had been able at last to tell the truth and take the weight of this terrible event off my shoulders by allowing somebody else to share it.

I guess what I really felt was relief. I told my husband that I felt exhausted, but relieved. As it was then about five o'clock in the evening he told me to sit down, watch the television and have a cuppa. I did and was eventually feeling OK. Then I went to the bathroom, washed my hands and looked up into the mirror. At that moment, horror of horrors, my nose started to bleed. Oh God, what's happening I thought, my thoughts racing, my heart pumping into my throat. I wanted to run — where to, I don't know. Fear was in me, all over me; what will I do; why is it happening again. I called out to my husband. I must have sounded terrible because he came running into the bathroom. I was standing there shaking and icy cold. It was happening and I felt that I just wanted to die now, right now, not later. My nose, the blood, the panic! He stayed calm, thank goodness, even though he must have been shocked at that sight again after all these years. He got ice packs and made me lie down on our bed, and for the first time in my life I admitted I was frightened.

I wanted my counselor, so my husband dialed the number and put the phone in my hand. In a moment she was on the other end and out it all came. I thought my father had come back and hit me on the head for telling. I was not regressing, but was reliving the power he had and my mother's threats — the blood, the fear. I was sure I was being punished until my counsellor talked to me about my greatest fear. Blood, why, what was happening?

Could they come back from the dead? No. Should I tell the truth? Yes. Did my father and mother use fear to control me and stop me from telling the truth about my life with my family? Yes. My answers were not those of a child. They were of an adult seeing the reason for me to have real fear at the time, but now seeing that I have nothing to fear. These people can no longer hurt me or control me and I am glad I have told the truth.

Now the nose bleeding is not a good experience, but having spoken to my counsellor I can understand what took place. My life was so horrendous that when I wrote of it and the terrible things I had seen and been involved in, I was there, even to the point of experiencing the smells, the sensations of pain and bleeding. It is not so unusual as it seems. It does happen in extreme cases like mine, I guess.

Another odd side to this happening is the fact that my counsellor, who is not prone to making up stories, told me that she had got a strange feeling at approximately 5 p.m. about me and was debating if she should call me or not. In my opinion, because it was all so unusual, I have no doubt in my mind that she got my subconscious call of fear and panic. This only substantiates my trust in this brilliant and caring person. It is now obvious to me how she guided me back to life. I will now travel again into my thoughts to try to show how I felt and saw things. As you will see many times throughout this book, I return to the past and back, often because this is the way it works. I hope the reader follows me without too much difficulty.

I remember now when my father returned early in the day and my mother did not expect him. It was odd because he would start whistling out the front, almost as a warning to her in case she had a man with her. It gave her time to shunt him out into the scrub. My father didn't seem to mind as long as the bed was empty when he walked in. As an adult now, I see it almost as if my father liked her to have men. He enjoyed the thought or the money, although she only spent it on clothes for herself, as far as I knew.

My father whistled a lot, but the horrible part of it was when I heard the sound change from one moment to a song; then he just whistled a strange, eerie, mournful sound and I knew it was going to be on. He and her were going to put me through the ropes again. My pain, their pleasure! When he whistled like that it was a warning and meant that he was in need of a distraction and I was it. My father had no mercy for me. His silence and his lack of love for his little girl was made more obvious to me each day of my life and will always be remembered by me.

I guess I dislike a lot of things because of my past life with my parents. Among these things is how I feel about other people and any families that have no abuse whatsoever. So what I dislike so much is when I hear people rubbish their parents for things that are so ordinary and human. It is so very important and intelligent to be able to see human error as one of the many faults we all suffer from and which we ourselves commit every day. We so often expect our parents to be the perfect image of our childlike dream. I wish I had been so lucky to have parents who just made mistakes like me and the rest of the world. It would have been beautiful to be loved by somebody who was human enough not to be perfect, but to be my mum and dad. How I envy them. They don't know how fortunate they are; it makes me very sad.

I remember the day very well when my father and mother were arguing about something and all of a sudden he picked me up by the arm and threw me against the wall. It hurt my head and I fell down on the floor. The lovely black velvet and sparkles came. The next thing I knew was he pulled me to my feet and I was sick. So he then started to punch my head very hard. I heard my mother telling him to stop, but by that time I didn't care — it was all black and flashing. I felt nothing. I was lying on the chaff bag mattress waiting for the ambulance to come.

Nothing worked — no arms, no legs, no hands, no feet, no voice, just eyes and tongue. She was kneeling at the foot of the bed and he was standing beside her. She was sort of praying, asking God to save her little girl. She was crying and big tears were running down her face, but I knew those tears were not for me. They were for herself, because she was afraid that the police would be told something bad had been going on in that house. It had turned against them at last. She knew when he was hitting me side to side on the head that she had waited too long before she told him to stop.

Dr Green said it looked as if my neck was broken and ordered me to hospital by ambulance. She still did not bother to clean me up, enough to pretend that I was cared for. They took me as I was — filthy dirty and in rags. My pretty curls were uncombed. When or how the ambulance got me there is not important, but it did take me to the Children's Hospital, Camperdown, Sydney, and even in my childhood confusion, I can still hear the nurses saying to each other: 'Come and have a look at the state of this child; look at the colour of her feet. God, look at her body, it's terrible.' The words live on today. I am still terrified of being taken to a hospital and not being able to bathe first. My time in the hospital is a little fuzzed up, but ice cream and jelly, white clean sheets and attention day and night stand out.

I do remember the ward, the iron cots, the sister at the desk near my bed, children coming and going, but not me although I didn't mind a bit. If it had been forever, that would have been OK by me. As it was, one day when I was about to eat my dinner, the nurse came to my cot with a big, big long box and said 'This is for you, Mary. Do you want to open it now or after dinner?' Of course, my answer was now and so it was the most beautiful moment in my life. I lifted the lid from the box. I could see inside the box — there was cellophane and, boy did my heart beat faster, the most beautiful doll I had ever seen! The nurse kept saying 'It's yours, Mary. Open it up and take it out.' I couldn't believe it. Finally, I did open the box further and touched the doll. She had dark hair, long legs and was so pretty with pink cheeks, creamy skin. I took her from the box and held her. What a moment!

There was a boy opposite me in the ward. He called out 'Let me see your dolly, Mary.' It was as if all the people knew and were happy for me. What a moment! To this day I can still feel the thrill and joy that I'd felt then in that hospital ward. This was no ordinary doll given to a sick kid. This one had been bought and paid for by the staff. They wanted it to be special, it was. If there was a God, he should have blessed them for what they did and for the joy they brought me — a joy so great that the memory still sends a thrill down my spine. Bless those nurses forever.

My parents did not visit me in hospital; the reason I do not know. On the day I was leaving the hospital my mother came for me. It was very warm and I remember the sun shining. After I was dressed and my mother did whatever she had to at the sister's desk, we started out of the ward and I kept telling my mother that I had to get my doll. She kept saying 'It's not your doll. It belongs to the hospital.' I was devastated. I believed what I saw and what I heard.

It was given to me new, not old like the other toys. I felt so sad, but then just as we were going through the door, the sister sang out 'Mary, wait you've forgotten your dolly.' I felt my little heart sing and I put out my arms, whereupon the sister put my doll in them. She said to me, 'That is your dolly to keep, Mary, and don't forget us.' I promised I wouldn't forget.

The doll had a name it was Babette. What a wonderful nurse she was to give me the beautiful doll, she was a saint and never knew what her kindness did for a little girl, it was powerful what she did. Even now years later, I cry when I think about my doll Babette.

The sad ending to this story of my doll came when I got married, and one day I asked my mother for my doll because by then I had a little girl called Michele. As Babette was so special, it was only natural that I wanted my own little live doll to have another pretty little companion.

However, my mother, true to her cruel and heartless ways with me, told me she had given the doll to my brother's little girl, and that was that. Oh how it hurt me. I had another scar now and my beloved Babette was gone, but not just gone anywhere. Even though I did not know this girl, I hated her. She had my lovely Babette and she was the daughter of one of my abuser brothers. How I hated her, even though she was probably unaware of the hurt it had caused me. My mother had done it again. She hurt me bad and to this day, I want Babette. She was mine, not my mother's and she did very much compensate me, for my pain. I would never forget her. She was mine. I had earned her the hard way. I was riddled with anger and still to this day, I am angry about the doll.

But there are other things I am angry about and they are things that affect all victims of abuse. The anger in me is strong. It is directed at the judicial system in this country. The hypocrisy of it, the fruitlessness, the pain it causes the victims of abuse. So many cases must be kept under wraps, never to come out into the open. The abusers are given a chance to protect themselves by this system, whereas the victim never gets this type of protection and but for this law, I would be able to expose the other abusers in my story, the other ones who sexually and physically assaulted me, and the others who mentally took away from me my rights to childhood and my name. They who put me through their sexual testing ground, their perverted abuse is still covered by law. I, the victim of their distorted minds, must consider them. I must make sure I do not destroy their names or their lives, as they destroyed mine.

Those of my abusers who are not dead know of their guilt and I know of their guilt, but I shall be working to see that there are changes made so that these people may also be made known before they die and so that they may pay for their crimes. It may be too late to take them to court and then to jail, but it's not too late to let the world see the type of animals they really are. The law gave me permission to confront them; the law said I have the right to tell my abusers that I remember what they did and that I cannot, and will not, ever forgive them. However, the law then said, but now don't tell anybody else, in case it causes them some trouble.

Where is the justice? Where is my protection? It wasn't there when these horrific things happened to me and it's not there now many years on into the world of law and order and caring people. A law to protect abusers — it sounds so bad to the ears of people like me; people who have never slept in gentle peace; people who never have the beautiful memories of being a child! What can I say to others like myself: don't worry, one day the criminal will serve their sentence, just like we have served ours. I say to other victims of abuse, our system is wrong, our laws are wrong, the abusers are wrong ... but we are right; we should have the right to name our abusers in public, not just quietly behind a piece of paper.

Let us in the future now stand up and be counted, let our numbers show and let our votes go to people who will protect us, as we were not ever before protected. It is up to us now to change these laws and publicly expose the criminals because as it is now, to give protection to these filthy-minded individuals, I must either leave them out of my book, or say that the characters in it are fictitious, and the places and people do not represent any living person!

It's hard for me to believe that I have lived almost my entire life in pain because of no help and the law tells me I must help the people who did it, so what else can I say to others? Well, I will say if we can survive the violence and sexual abuse that we have endured, then we will survive this insult as well, except we will not allow it to go on. We must break this wall of protecting the guilty and show that from all of us out here we will stand up and protect ourselves. This is our country, too; it does not just belong to the abusers. It will be up to us to make the changes to protect others from this terrible piece of injustice.

Imagine the number of people out there who, like myself, could never talk about what had happened to them; the people who through the trauma of abuse, locked it out of their lives within their own system — a system that also takes away their living skills, the skills that would normally tell them it's OK to cry, it's OK to say No, and allow them to see that they are worth loving; that they should have respect for themselves. Well, I am sure that the number of people would be incredibly high. So the amount of pain that is not documented because of the law, must be far greater than the people of this country wish to admit to.

The law does not allow you to say who your abusers were. You can't say they were your brothers, if you had any; or if they were your neighbours, if you had any; or uncle or aunts, if you had any. It hinges on threats of silence that kept you from telling when you were young. You know what I mean: 'Don't tell or else', it does sound familiar, doesn't it? How are we going to convince people that it's OK to tell, if the law says No, it's not OK.

Now, if the abuser is dead, that's OK, or if they're in jail, it's OK, but if you can't take them to court because of the time lapse, and you can't publicly accuse them, or publicly talk about it, what are we all talking about?

The law tells me that I must remain silent about these people, so for the moment, I will obey the law. I would like to think that my story is a one only and that no other child or adult was put through the torment of everlasting pain. But even as I write, I realise that it is not so, and that out there, in this educated world of ours there are other stories of acts of perversion carried out against other people, that silence surrounds the victim and the person who carried it out. But let us hope that as each story emerges from the closet, we will be closer to a solution.

The funny thing (or not so funny) about all this is that you would think that I'd hate bread today, but that is not so. I really like bread and butter; it's one of my favourite foods. Sometimes when I hear my father say: 'She's the Bread and Butter Queen', that can make me stop eating it for a while, but then I start back on it and I am OK.

If a soldier, policeman or fireman is wounded, they are heroes and justly rewarded. But if you have been wounded as a child of abuse, there are only a handful of people who care. This must change. I can see that it will never become a major issue for the world, but if we want to help our country, then we must protect our children. The people who took away my innocence and childhood went to extremes to convince all they came into contact with, that I was some vile contaminated creature without morals and, of course, not to be believed or trusted, or listened to, because if I was listened to they themselves would have to be judged. So my silence was imperative to them. As you can now see, I am not silent anymore about my life, but I will obey the law. Why, I don't know.

I remember when I found it easy to say nothing, I stopped talking and why not? I know I was thirteen — the doctor told me I was — and nobody listened anyway, so there was no point in speaking. Babette (my doll) always listened, but never spoke.

They took me to Canterbury Hospital. There was a lady doctor at the hospital and she spoke to me alone for a long time, asking me questions about home and my not talking. She said there was nothing wrong in my throat, so it was in my mind. Why didn't I want to talk? Then I did talk to her, but I was too clever to tell her what was going on. I wanted to live and if I told, they really might kill me, I thought. She then sent me out and called them in. Shit, she should have been smarter than that, I thought. After all, she was a doctor and they're supposed to be smart. The silly, stupid bitch told my mother and father that I had told her some things and she was worried about me. As soon as we got outside the hospital and started to walk home, he looked at me and said 'You stupid bastard, wait till I get you home.'

It was a long walk at any time from Canterbury Road, Campsie, to Chullora, but that day it was longer and more than frightening. Each step of the way I was trying to work out how I could run away, or fall down a gully or something and I was hating that doctor. I didn't tell her anything important, so why did she do what she did? Why couldn't she have just said that she thought there was something wrong. I thought if I had nice big brothers they would save me, but I didn't, so that was that.

Always planning, always worried and always waiting. Life really was bad sometimes. The evening light was fading when the fat man arrived. He was laughed at by my family for his grotesque size and looks, but he was there for me. My father had arranged for him to have me with a view to marriage. It was getting closer to my being got rid of and married.

The man stunk of alcohol and was quite drunk. My father handed him a blanket and suggested he and I go to a place called 'Devil's Den' out back from us. It was so named because of the tall dark trees and the silence of the place. We did not walk far because the fat one was too drunk and even when sober, I doubt if he could have walked that far. He put the blanket on the ground and we sat on it. Then he lay down like a big whale and whatever he planned was out. He started to vomit and, luckily for me, he was very sick. After about an hour we walked back. In his sick state he said something to my father and my father told him off. I never saw him again, lucky me.

When I got close to 14 years the beatings almost came to a halt. I guess it would be seen and the bleeding from the nose kept happening. It interfered with their pleasure. My father still had sexual intercourse with me and when he finished, he would pull his penis out and let the semen run over my stomach. Then he would say 'Go and wash yourself, you dirty slut. Have a look at yourself in the mirror. I won't even be able to sell you to a wino, you dirty moll.'

Somehow I could now see that it was getting time for me to start finding a way out before it was too late. One evening he had asked her what they should do with me because I would start beginning to get smart. I heard them talk of the white slave market, but did not understand that at all. However, it must have done something in my head because from then on I wanted out. How though, and I was so much of a slut — where do sluts go or who with? I was scared and very confused. I knew my time was nearly up, so I did leave home eventually. They did not want me to stay and I wanted to get away from them, but had nowhere to go except to strangers. Only being about 15 years old, it was a little difficult since they would not help me in any way at all.

My mother and father eventually found a job for me with Allen's Private Hotels at Neutral Bay. There I was in a little cold room under the hotel, put into service. all by myself for the first time in my life with a job of trust and honour. It's just a pity that I did not fully understand any of it except to be out of that prison called 'home'.

Now fortunately for me, I met a young woman from Russia who I think may have been a cook and lived in another one of the basement rooms. She did not speak a lot of English, but she was very kind to me because she said that I was too young to be working in a private hotel, and tried to show me how to survive. I will never forget her kindness to me. She introduced me to her friends, two very big wrestlers. They also treated me like their little friend. I was amazed at the way they were. It was not until many,

many years later that I found out in the papers she was to become one of Sydney's well-known, notorious characters and prostitutes. Her life was always centered on East Sydney and Central Police Station, almost the same spots that I spent much of my terrifying childhood. It was more than a little uncanny, but to me she was a kind person whom I did not ever forget.

Sadly for me, my experience as a housemaid only lasted about a year, until I foolishly took a ring from one of the rooms that I was responsible for cleaning. How I regretted that foolish action because up till that moment I had not done anything like that. I never touched anything in the rooms. I was quiet and did my job. Nobody had ever complained about me, or my work, but it was a lovely little ring with a red stone in it and I was tempted. Instead of thinking of the seriousness of my actions, I took it, never thinking that I was doing something illegal. Where were my brains? And, of course, after work I went into my Russian friend's room, just like I did each evening as I had not learned how to go out or things like that.

When I told her and showed her the ring, she got really upset. She said she was upset at me for doing something so bad and that I was now a thief, not the nice little quiet girl she thought I was. I said I would take it back in the morning and she said good, it was the right thing to do. The next morning the first thing I did was to take the ring and put it back where I took it from. Unknown to me, though, it had already been reported missing and within a few moments of returning it to the room, my lady boss called me into her office. There was another young woman with her, the owner of the ring. The boss said, 'Mary, we think you stole a ring from Miss so and so. You were the only one who has been in her room and it's gone now. What have you got to say for yourself?'

Well, I felt sick and being very shy and withdrawn, I just stood there. Perhaps I was waiting to be hit or something, I don't really know what I was expecting. So as usual, I said nothing; no explanation of my actions or the fact that I had returned the ring a few minutes earlier. Then the lady boss said she had no choice, but to call the police. I guess my silence was my confession. The lady excused herself saying she would be available for the police when they arrived. Meanwhile, I just stood there in the office waiting for the police. They arrived and there were two of them. Questions were asked about my age and job. They had just asked me if I had taken the ring when before I could answer, the lady came back smiling saying 'Stop, it's all right. I have my ring back. It was on the dressing table where it had been when I last saw it. Let the little girl go, she didn't take it after all.' The policemen said 'Good, all's well that ends well.' But the boss said, 'No, wait a moment.'

'Did you take the ring or not Mary?'

So I told them the whole story, why and when I had put it back and that I had made a mistake for which I was sorry. The lady said she was pleased with my ability to put it back and apologise to her. The police said it was a very good thing what I had done in owning up and they didn't feel I would do it again.

I said I would not as I wanted to keep my job. However, the boss lady said she wanted to teach me a good lesson and uphold the standard of the hotel. The police were angry with her because what could they charge me with? The ring was back, but she said she wanted me out and taught a lesson, so that was that. The police, therefore, took me to a children's shelter saying they were not happy and were sorry, but the lady was the boss and they had to do their job.

Wow! Women sure were my enemies. I did not understand what was going on, but I knew I was in trouble. The shelter was terrible. Why it was called that, I'll never know. It was a little hell hole, not a shelter.

I had a medical examination by a dirty old man without a heart. He was more than a little shocked at the condition of my body and asked a million questions, but I answered none. I knew, once more, it was better to shut up. Telling the truth got you nowhere.

So they notified each child's parents to come, but mine took four days. When they finally did arrive, I was taken before the judge, who was more than a little curious about me. He told my parents that there was no case against me, but he was of the opinion that I was not capable of being out in the workforce alone and that I needed the protection of a family until I was older. He felt I was childlike and immature and was sending me home for my parents to protect me. Oh hell, why didn't he just have me shot! I went home with them in silence. It was just like when I used to run away and the police always sent me back. They must have all been blind. My life took up exactly the same as it was when I had left. No more beltings, but insults and degrading acts, so I tried to live in silence and not be noticed, hoping they would leave me alone each day, a million hours long, and the nights waiting

I then went to a live-in job at Strathfield where I nursed young children. It was then that my father said, 'I've got you a husband, you're getting married in a few weeks.' Until my marriage to this man, I only met him once with my mother and father. I remember one of the neighbours of his family being introduced to me. She held my hand very

Teenage Mary

tightly and said 'Don't marry into that family, you'll be very sorry. You're a child and don't know them.' How I wish I had the brains to have listened to that lady.

It was raining the day I married him. I wore a blue suit that his mother has chosen for me to wear, together with the hat and shoes. My father wore a bow-tie and smoked a big cigar in the Baptist church at Burwood. "After all, she said, this is my son's wedding" and she was in charge, choosing everything, I was only his wife! He was well paid by my father and as a gambler it was well received and soon gone and I belonged to the Buchanan family.

When the wedding ceremony was finished my father stood up and said 'Thank God that's done, money well spent.'

We spent our wedding night on a bed outside the toilet door on the back verandah. The family thought it was a good idea. It didn't worry me because I was married and that was that. I would never have to go home again, so that was good. However, nobody told me what marriage was about. I was going to learn the hard way and, as they said, 'I'd made my bed, now I would have to lie in it.'

In a few short weeks I was to be in hospital paying the price of marriage to that man. My husband was afraid only of his mother and made me promise that I would tell her I was a virgin. I really didn't know what he meant by a 'virgin'. The only one I'd ever heard of was the Virgin Mary from the church and it was a name, not a condition.

When my first daughter was born, my husband came to the hospital (the Roslyn Private Hospital at Arncliffe) to see for his mother what the child looked like. She had told me that they only liked blue-eyed blonde-haired girls. No boys wanted, and no brown eyes or olive skins like mine. So my little girl was like them with very fair blue eyes, everything they ordered, and on the day I took her home, they had visitors over to see 'his baby', as they called her. His mother very firmly informed me that this was her son's baby, not mine, and if I ever thought of leaving, it would not be with the baby.

She belonged to them, even though he was not even interested in the child. His mother was the boss of all things and she took control of everything. The woman looked like a lady; she sang Salvation Army hymns all the time; she dressed up as if she was somebody and worked in the city at a store called Farmers. When she came home in the evening she pulled dozens of pairs of silk stockings out of her underwear, which she had stolen each day to sell from home. This was another 'Christian act'.

She told me one day she was very good at abortions and had performed as many as 29 of them on her own daughter, even to having had to break the infants into pieces to get them out. She also told me that she would kill for her son (my husband) and warned me often that she could destroy me if she wanted to. I believed her!

She had a boarder, and his wish was her command. The best of the food went to him. If he wanted her, he just clicked his fingers. I, too, became his part-slave, though not as a lover. He would come home drunk at all hours and many, many times tell her to get the kid (me) out of bed. So I would have to sing for him and his friends in the lounge room. Even in late pregnancy he would do this to me at 1, 2, 3, 4 o'clock in the morning just to sing.

How I hated it! My husband was too afraid of his mother to protect me. I formed an attachment to his sister, many years older than me. She was a married woman with a child from a previous lover and a child from her husband. She was, I thought, my new sister, my friend, my confidante — and my downfall, as I found out too late.

Approximately two months into my marriage I was transported by ambulance to Prince Alfred Hospital with internal injuries inflicted through my husband's insatiable sexual behaviour. This provoked jokes, fun and laughter from the family. My husband wore it like a badge of honour. What a man! Once I did tell his mother that my life with him was hell. Her answer was 'He is just like his father was.' She said she had divorced him for his terrible sexual behaviour. She also said that when Lyall was a boy, she had found her son on many occasions performing terrible sexual acts, but did not tell me what they were.

As I've said, my next mistake was to confide in his sister. She was sympathetic and said she knew her brother was a bit of an animal and that I deserved better treatment. Her idea was that she had a boyfriend at work who had a friend that she wanted me to meet. He was an Italian man, single, tall, kind and it would be OK because she and her boyfriend would be there with me always. She said her brother Lyall would not mind seeing as who I was, together with my way of living and thinking. This must have been all right, she was his sister and was old. So it all took place and I met him. We went with her and her boyfriend to Villawood Hostel where we talked. In front of me, she told him that her brother was a monster and they said what a terrible thing for me to have to go through. This man was kind and did not ask for anything, even when she and her bloke started to have sex in front of us. I thought he was a gallant knight there to protect and care for me. I was surely in heaven at last and he was handsome, whereas my husband was positively not. So it all began.

Then just after I gave birth to my third beautiful dark-eyed, dark-haired son, I discovered that the man who supposedly loved me and wanted to take me away and marry me, was already married, which had been arranged by proxy to his childhood promised bride. My husband, sister in-law and all the family knew. I found out the day I went to his new house which I thought he was buying for US. I saw the photo of a new baby, about the same age as my baby.

His wife had been in Australia for some time, and we had both been pregnant about the same time. When I saw the photo I asked him who it was and he told me that it was his wife, but added that we could still go on together as always. Even my poor hurt brain could see now for the first time that it was all wrong. No one had indicated that it was wrong. Even my husband said it was OK; his family said it was OK.

But now, poor mixed up defeated Mary said it's not OK! It was over and at last after so many mistakes.

Bad men and violence were my life by now. I never even dreamed that there was another way to live and who would show me the way? By now my hard life was taking its toll as I went from one bad situation to the next. If only there had been just one person to show me what was wrong. I had the brain, but this was not enough. I needed help in so many ways and many other things were wrong.

At one stage, while living at Strathfield with my husband's family, I could not walk without falling over. His mother mocked me always and kept saying I was seeking attention. It was very bad. After about 10 months of this, they had all gone away to Brisbane for a holiday leaving me, and my tiny baby girl alone with nothing except a tin of condensed milk. The beautiful neighbour, who had begged me not to marry into the family and cried on my wedding day, saw a light on and came over and found us. They were beautiful kind people and looked after us until the family returned from their holidays in Queensland.

However, I was still not able to stand without falling over, so I was forced to seek medical attention. I went to a doctor in Burwood Road who was concerned about me. After some short time he put me in Highbury Hospital, Wentworth Road, Strathfield, where he and another fine doctor, his son, operated on me in the hope it would help me to walk. They were both curious, but I never talked ... It was obvious to them there was a story to be told, but I wouldn't tell. All this was a by-product of cruelty. I would pay (again) and my dear children, too, would pay very much for my lack of living skills and own childhood (my biggest regret).

Nevertheless, if you were to ask me what was good in my life, I would have to say my children because my dear little children were the only real things that I'd ever had and the fleeting memory of that darling little girl who had gone. This I would pay for all the rest of my life and so would she.

When my eldest child, a girl, was about five years old and my first son was about one year old, I was pregnant again with my second little girl. During this time my husband still had sex with me, even though he'd told his mother he was not, of course he hadn't told her that the baby had been conceived when he'd made me have sex with a man in payment for a gambling debt while he watched. When my baby was on the way, he told me that it would have to go because his mother wouldn't be happy with him. I did not believe him nor even think once about what he had said and even when he went to the Salvation Army people to make arrangements, it did not register in my poor sick head that this could happen!

The day after my baby was born, he took me from the hospital at Paddington straight to the Salvation Army at Marrickville and made me leave my little baby there for the night. He said the neighbours must not see her, so I would have to tell everybody she was dead. Still I did not believe it was happening and so I did just what I was told. The next morning he said we had to hurry back to the hospital and pick up the baby. I was thrilled and felt that everything was going to be all right. I was to get my little baby back. I knew he couldn't do it. She was innocent; I was happy.

So away we went and picked my little one up. We continued on into the city. That seemed OK. I thought we would change trains and return to Villawood on another line. However, we got out at Wynyard, not Central, and started to walk for quite some distance till we entered an old building. I was curious, but not worried. I had my baby in my arms and that was the main thing. We went into a pokey little waiting room with a young woman sitting behind a little desk. She seemed to know my husband's name. We just sat there and in a couple of minutes the young woman went into another room. Then she came back, walked briskly over to us, reached down, took my baby as if to admire her and walked back through the door to the other room. I don't know if I felt anything because it couldn't have been happening. She was gone ... my baby was gone ... I was Mary, but nobody listened to Mary! Where was my baby? Didn't I have a baby or was it the girl's behind the desk. I turned to Lyall wanting him to say that she would be back in a moment, but instead he said 'Come on, get out of here.' and pulled me out of the door. He walked in front of me, back to the station.

My husband's sick idea to punish me and the children was to give me two shillings a day on which to feed the family. This was because he and his mother would go to the races and spend most of their money, leaving very little money to exist on. Another one of his ways to win sympathy was to sleep on the house steps either front or back, so that the neighbours would think I had locked him out, and if he gained sympathy, I would have no voice against him.

How I wish I had been as clever as him, but I was neither clever nor a liar. I had no chance of beating him then and besides, he always had his mother to cover for him. I stood alone between him and his mother. They changed the life of my daughters. How I wish there had been someone to show me the way; to stand up to them and stop all that cruelty going on in my life and make me see that what I was doing was all wrong. If only I could just learn how to stop this happening. What was wrong with me?

I can see a lot of things now that weren't right and what was wrong with me back then. I had no living skills at all; no training in right and wrong; no understanding of my own worth and no defence. I have never known how to fight. I just knew how to stay alive. Saying no was not possible for me as I'd never been allowed to use this word and didn't even want to. I just wanted to be wanted and even though it was bad, it was better than nothing, I thought.

I went from a family that didn't love me or show affection towards me, other than perverted, to another family that didn't love me or show any affection and a man who didn't love me. I had stopped crying very early in life to prevent any further punishment. Then I couldn't cry because of ridicule from this family. It was a vicious circle. I had entered a family that didn't kiss, hold, cuddle or show any affection even to each other, so it was set in concrete and in my mind there was no such thing as love.

But that is changing. In my life now I am happy to say that I can cry; it's wonderful and I am not afraid to show that I feel hurt or happy. My tears do not bring me punishment and I never really knew how wonderful tears were.

CHAPTER SIX

Now I must take you back again to Villawood, and show you how I was surviving with the children and my husband.

By now I was very sick and suffering from malnutrition. My neighbours gave me a little food for the children. He didn't even want to feed the sweet little girl who looked like him, let alone the ones who were referred to as the 'black bastards'. There was no heart in that family.

The children were not to blame, but were treated as outcasts. I would never let the children out of my sight and over-protected them and watched them all day. I hand sewed pieces of material and made beautiful clothes for them. The neighbours paid me to sew for them and my pride was my little girl, for whom I would sew little pieces of lace together and make pretty dresses for her. With her endowment I bought a hair ribbon, socks and pants. She looked like a little doll, her curls tied with a pretty bow and always sweet, clean and protected. I loved it when people commented on my children's well-cared for appearance. I have never beaten, molested or abused my children, nor allowed them to be abused. I would have killed myself first.

One day my husband took my five-year-old son down to the corner of the main road and sent him across to the shop in the afternoon peak hour traffic. My poor baby never had a chance. A truck hit him and he suffered brain damage. The doctors at Fairfield Hospital said there was not much chance. His head was as big as a balloon and his colour was green.

I sat alone, pregnant with Leo, about eight months. It was the high point of horror for me. No one cared, only me, plus a couple of nuns, but no family, only me. Why were my children paying such a high price for their bad mother, I thought.

The policeman who lived in my street came to the house to ask about the accident. He said 'I did not believe it was one of your children hit by the truck. They are the only kids in the street kept in their own yard and looked after so well.' He said he could not believe that an adult would be so stupid as to send a baby across the main road in heavy traffic. He and the rest of my street were very upset for me, but no member of the family visited the hospital to see him. He lived, my son.

All of my children, though not arriving with love, warmth, flowers or even a visitor to the hospital, were my beautiful babies, I thought God was trying to make up for the lost childhood I had been deprived of. I wanted each pretty little bundle. I didn't care what people said or did to me — I was nothing — but my babies were my life. This was to be the family I had wanted so badly.
I would love them; they would love me. I wouldn't hurt them; they wouldn't hurt me. My life was going to turn around, or so I thought.

I did have a very dear friend whom I had met at St Therese School, Lakemba. She was to save my life. Her real name is Patricia. She would knit pretty woolens for my little ones and pop in, cuddle them and beg me to move out of that house of torment. She always turned up and gave her beautiful friendship to us. She was a pretty little blue-eyed blonde with a nature as sweet as her looks.

One day when she came there was no food in the house and I had on the only clothes I owned. She looked at me and pleaded with me to leave. I was afraid as apart from her, I had no one. At least there I had a Housing Commission home to live in.

But I was dying, and I guess I knew it, but thought if I kept going, I could, perhaps, beat it. However, my beautiful friend was determined and even threatened never to come again if I did not leave with the children there and then. She said my babies would have no mother at all if I did not get out. So I accepted her help and caring heart, but where to?

As a result of my lifestyle, my body had been well and truly abused. Through lack of proper food, no rest and five children after years of abuse from childhood till 29 years old, I suffered many things, but now I was to be intravenously fed and treated for the effects and damage done by malnutrition.

I was devastated! What do you do with four children that nobody wants? Patricia had to work and my husband's family hated the boys. His mother wanted my little girl, even though her father did not. I was desperate. I approached many Christian organisations, but nobody wanted them. The Welfare would have them if I gave them up and they would be sent off in different directions. So as I got sicker, my worry got bigger. My darling Patricia wanted to help and wanted to cheer me up. I was beyond cheering up by now. I'd had so many things confusing me ... with my illness, weighing in at six stone and at five foot nine inches tall, I must have looked grotesque, but she begged a lady to mind my babies for a week so that I could compose myself and prepare to die, I think.

After a couple of days I decided that my dear little girl should not be denied a chance to live in a family, perhaps not good, but they would not hurt her, I thought, as my mother-in-law was always saying that my daughter belonged to them, not me. I spoke to my husband. He didn't show much interest, but his mother got smart and said I was a good mother making the very best decision any mother could make. I was sacrificing my feelings and placing my little girl before myself. I needed this push and I believed her. I was certainly not worldly-wise or cunning, so it was easy for my husband and his mother to outwit me in the sneakiest possible way. So when I asked my daughter, who was nine years old and aware that her Mummy was sick, how she felt about living with Daddy and Nana, her first answer was No. Then my husband offered her five pounds a week pocket money as against none from Mummy. She was just a little girl after all, so she changed her mind and said she wanted to live with Daddy. I felt like the lady in the Bible who gave up her baby to prevent having her cut into halves, and my big dream was that when my girl knew of my sacrifice, she would love me more.

But I under-estimated my in-laws. In no time at all I became the enemy. They never told her the truth of my love. The mother-in-law did exactly what she had threatened earlier in my married life, that she would get my child because she was fair, not dark like me and was theirs, not mine. I begged my sister-in-law to tell her the truth, but it was a waste of time. She also had nearly lost her child to her own mother. She was afraid of her just as my husband was.

The story has no happy ending. I had to place my boys in Woodlands Boys' Home at Newcastle. Provided I paid, took them out and clothed them I thought they would be safe altogether. This was another mistake they paid for.

I have since discovered that my middle son was regularly sexually abused by the visiting Christians and my other two sons don't say anything at all. So my children have also paid very dearly for my abused mind. It just snow-balled. I see now how many were destroyed by my family; how the effects through me and my loss of identity turned their darling lives around. You cannot assume children will get over it or grow up through it. I cannot assume anything, I never have, but I did hope for better things for my children.

Thank goodness there is help today for mothers who are in trouble. In my day, if you left your husband, you needed a family to turn to because there was no unmarried mothers support scheme; no rental assistance. There was, of course, the Child Welfare Department and if you went to them, they helped by taking your children and placing them in care, as they called it, orphanages, foster homes separated from each other, and your chances of getting them back were as slim as their chances of ever being together again.

If you went to the police, as I did, you wasted your time. The policeman was just that: a man, same sex as your husband. I was told by the sergeant to go home and that my place was with my husband. 'After all,' he said, 'are you going to walk out every time the going gets tough? He was working for you, wasn't he? And he did have conjugal rights, you know. Anyway, love, you made your bed, now you must lay in it. Go on now, that's a girl, off you go.' That may sound pretty unrealistic compared with today's help, but it is true.

I remember way back when a woman I knew asked me to go to Melbourne with her and said we could get jobs, work and keep ourselves and I could support my daughter, who was at that time my only child. So I planned to go, but could not take her with me and unfortunately there was no one who would mind her for me until I had a job and somewhere to live. My friend suggested one of my abusers who was married and had a child of his own then. I had not told her of my abused childhood or the fact that this person was one of my abusers 'Ben'. I was in a spot, but my way of working it out was the fact that he now had a wife and child of his own, he did not need my girl, so I asked them. They said yes.

I did get a job in a lolly factory and asked my girl friend's fiancé's brother if he could pick up my daughter while in Sydney and bring her to me. He was kind and said he would. I gave him a letter of introduction to the people who had my girl, which explained it all. He picked her up and came straight down to me with her. I thought I was on the way to a good life.

Then I discovered this man only wanted to use me. So back to Sydney and to my husband I went. I paid the price of a young woman not prepared for life, its dangers, its pitfalls or the cunning people who prey on vulnerable women, unskilled in life and only to be used and abused.

I received no help from the society in which I lived — just condemnation from every avenue. My mind was too confused and I was completely alone, my husband and his family were the only ones I could go to. I had no knowledge of what was good or bad.

Most girls are taught certain skills by their mothers, such as cooking, sewing, mothering. These skills were not made available to me. There was no role model for me to learn from; no mother to ask advice of, so I was a sure thing to make many mistakes and I sure did that.

One of my mistakes was to believe that if I was the opposite of my parents, such as to give unquestioning love, it would be returned. Give all of yourself and sacrifice your wishes for them; put no limitations on their wishes.

The mistakes were piling up, all in the name of what I thought was good mothering. I had beautiful children and that I thought was God's gift to me to make up for deserting me when I had needed him most during my childhood. They were very special and they were my own family. I would love them and they would love me in return. They were going to replace the empty gap in my heart; a real family, no pain, no hurt, no cruelty, always together, always loving me as much as I loved them. There was no thought in my mind that people would look upon my babies as black bastards as my mother-in-law called them. They were not black, even though their hair was. Neither were they bastards, nor were they inferior or born of unwed parents. As for the physical fathers of my children, I did not understand nor think wrong of this. I sincerely believed what I said earlier: that they were gifts from God and he was making up to me for the pain I had suffered.

But there were many things that were hard to understand, such as where do the instincts of motherhood come from? What made me love my little babies so much? I remember my little girl when she was born — my first girl — even though I had been told she wasn't mine and that she would never be, I was so proud of this little blonde with the big blue eyes and no matter what happened in her life, she was mine always; that's what I felt and when the neighbours where I lived used to say how beautifully I kept her, I felt happiness like I had never felt before. My love for her showed — it was in her pretty blonde curls that were always shiny and had pretty ribbons tied on them. I guess after all she was my blonde Babbette and love was a foreign word to me, but this had to be love because it was unselfish, tender and caring. Where did it come from? How did it happen? What made me ever unable to hurt my little babies after being brought up only knowing pain and sorrow? Why didn't I just continue the pattern, why?

I am only a plain and simple cook, but where did I learn to cook at all; where did I learn to keep my home spotlessly clean as well as wash and iron? How did I know how to talk tenderly to my little boys and also how was it so easy for me to love being a mother; to love the problems and poverty it all brought? The joy my children brought me was the greatest joy in my entire life. Each of them was special — my little girls, so very fair and delicate as flowers, and my little boys so handsome with dark flashing eyes and shiny black silky curls. What a reward for a person lost in confusion and pain!

I've never regretted having them; I hope they haven't regretted it either. Once again, you can see that I slip back and forth with my story. But I hope you are still with me.

My story is like my life was: uneven and disjointed, but once again I'll try to explain that each day as I sit down and write, I think what it would have been like. If I could type, especially with more than one finger, it sure would have been easier than writing by hand which is what I have done. I printed each word so that when the time came to transfer it into draft form and put all the different sections in the right order, it would be easier for someone to understand. I could not write it as if it was a simple straight forward story; I could only write it as I was able to handle it which meant that each section I wrote may have been days, months or even years apart so they were not in book form from the beginning. I then had to be able to reassemble each of these sections into their right position in this book, or it would have been just mixed up and very hard to follow. So for me it was an exercise in learning another thing about myself.

I found I needed strength and honesty, together with the ability to look at myself as I really was; the discipline to come back to the book each day — and sometimes in the night — when I knew that it could be more painful. But I did it; I have discipline and have still have the courage I had as a child.

This is what made this story not just another book on abuse. I have put my life into writing this book, my sad and private thoughts, my pain and my right to remain just a voice in the wilderness. I hope it helps people understand the effort put into this book, so that they may know about me.

There are things that I remember when I had the children. I would watch the other mothers receive flowers and visitors, all beaming with admiration for them. It was a little bit sad for me because I truly did not understand why nobody wanted to come and visit me and admire my babies.

Each time was the same. The nurses and doctors were very kind and paid me many compliments about my pretty babies, but it would have been nice to have somebody tell me that I had done a good job; that they were proud of me and brought pretty gifts for them. But I suppose if I had not been so naive or unaware of my predicament, I would have known that in the eyes of many people, I had been judged guilty without the benefit of a trial. So my little babies were punished too, though they were also innocent of any crime. It was not fair, but it is the way of the people and this was the continuing saga of abuse, always striving to do what is right, but with no guide lines to show you.

So instead of help, criticism and intolerance were your only guidelines.

Of course, it's much easier to criticise a person than to reach out with help. To be surrounded by people who were themselves guilty of complete and utter disregard for the feelings of others made it impossible to be helped to overcome the total loss of self-esteem and be shown the correct skills of living.

Sometimes I have been so exhausted, so washed out from

putting on my mask, that even to eat was too much of an effort. My situation became one of pretending that it was no effort for me to be the slave of those who wished to use me, while hoping that I would be loved for my kindness, always looking for crumbs.

Love in childhood is, I am sure, the basis for good living in later life. We should all have it.

Oh how I wish I could write each and every thought that enters my mind. There are so many of them, such as the distance that I have travelled since birth; the roads so rough and long and here I am writing about it for all to see. It's a bit like living in a house with no blinds — you are vulnerable, you are exposed to criticism and even to ridicule.

I realize that by writing about my silent pain, I will once again have to accept the fact that there are many people who do not have the ability to care for others or to feel their pain, and most of all to be able to confront issues that they themselves have difficulty coming to terms with. But this is a small price to pay really when all things are considered, and when I think how much it has helped me. I now live with the knowledge that I am a person, not a worthless thing to be used and abused by anybody and that I am in control of my life. So what is good for me and causes me no pain is what I am entitled to.

The feeling of power that I have is wonderful.

Each day I see instances where I make decisions; that I never would have done before. As I write each page, I see changes in the way I think about things; how I react to people and their demands, plus my ability to stand firm on my beliefs and not allow others to force their ideals onto me. I have ideals of my own now and I will make sure I do my best to reach them. I no longer live behind the mask I created. This is me; not perfect, but I like it and it's a damn shame I missed such a lot of it. As they say 'Better late than never.' The human mind sure is a wonderous thing.

I always felt it was a shame I did not get the opportunity and encouragement to be educated, but if you want to learn, you will. I proved that to myself — all you have to do is listen. And remember another thing do not be afraid anymore. You don't have to be. I know this is true because I am an example of someone who was afraid and with no self-esteem at all. Each day was hell. Now today is better because I will not let somebody stand over me in any way.

However, there are people out there who think that victims are what they are because (1) they like the attention; (2) they didn't want to stop; (3) They are making big issues out of nothing. These people think that you just put it behind you and that's that. I know this to be true because I have heard these people in clubs, social gatherings, shopping centers. Each time I heard them I closed my mouth tighter convinced that I could never speak. Now I suggest to all survivors, close your ears to people who cannot, or will not, face their own inability to come to terms with abuse. Maybe they were or are abused people themselves and cannot face the pain like you and I have done. Do not allow yourself to be hurt or put down by these people. You, above all, can understand their confusion, but they, too, must understand yours.

Now, no matter what you think, my book is not a book of therapy, even though it does touch on this subject quite often. It is my own conclusion to many of the problems faced by victims of abuse. I hope that it will give insight into this distorted world of pain and loneliness in which people like me live and also show the many ways we conceal it. The older victims of abuse, such as myself, are the unheard of ones, because there is very little, if any, discussion on us. As you get older, it does not mean that the pain or memory gets less or the devastating effects wear off. I would say that it gets worse if anything, because for me it did.

I could see what it had done to my life and relationships; what it had done to my family with regard to the carry-on effect. Each day I would see a reminder of my destructive childhood and living to old age with this horror inside me, is the same as living with a monster and not having anyone recognise it as such. I did not want to die with this terrible story still concealed inside me. My penalty for being born into my family was like a lifetime in a prison within myself. Sixty years is a long time to serve and more so, if you are innocent. What is the compensation? Can there be any? Who do I sue? Who pays? How much can I ask? Do I claim for loss of limb or do I claim for loss of life? So will it help if I can claim and can a miracle turn back the clock to prevent it happening to me? No it can't, but we can help prevent it happening again, if we want to. We are the people who have the power.

Let us together stand up and demand changes in the courts. Let us show them that abuse is not just another crime. It is not a cut and dried situation. It is different to all other crimes because, mostly, there is no witness and the victim cannot talk or the perpetrator is an upright citizen of the community with no criminal record or above reproach in every way — a smiling mother, a protective father or protective older brothers. Anybody may be an abuser.

While writing this I was thinking that maybe people feel only the female is the victim of sexual abuse or that only the little girls and little boys suffer the indignity of being played with. FULL STOP!

Well, my book is for all victims of abuse and that, sure as hell, includes little boys, big boys, young men and let's not forget older men.

Have any of you heard of rape? Well your answer is yes, I know that. But what about rape of a male? It's happening all the time and we don't even give it a thought. If you did, it would make you sick with horror. The male who goes through rape is in physical pain from injuries to his anal area, tearing, bleeding — pain that won't let up. They experience the same mental anguish and destruction as a female, but with less sympathy. 'Take a pain killer, it will heal up.' These are the familiar words that male victims hear. Does he cry? Does he hide from the world and himself? And what about his relationships with other men or women friends — does he really have nightmares like us?

Yes he does, and yes he cries, and yes he needs the same help as women. So take notice, because may be there is somebody in your life who needs help and tender care. It maybe a male, not a female.

Recovery will never be complete unless we start to see the tragedy of rape and abuse to both sexes, not just one. Men cry, too, and take up substances for support and then the problem escalates in the same way as it does in women. We will look and we will care — you are not alone anymore and will make society see your pain, your terror.

As I mentioned before, when I was a child my walk indicated that there was something wrong. Other children had no scruples about commenting on this or making fun of me for it. So I cultivated a walk that would hide my pain and at the same time, make me look like everybody else. It paid off because I remember suffering terrible spinal problems and being in St Joseph's Hospital, Auburn. They told me that I might have to go into a full body cast for some time. My very sweet neighbour had been minding my children as nobody else would look after them for me. However, she had about five of her own, so it was too much for her. When she came to the hospital and told me that none of my family or relatives would take care of them, I grew very desperate.

The fear of the Welfare taking them pushed me to ask the specialist if I could go home. He laughed and asked how. I said I would walk, but he was so sure I couldn't that he turned to the sister next to him and said, 'If she can walk, I'll carry her bag to the door myself.' I repeated it and said to him 'OK. Can I go home if I can walk across the room?' and he said 'Yes, you can go home if you can walk five steps.' So even though I was flat on my back and in pain to be sure, I remembered walking. I told myself to do it and I would feel no pain. Well, it worked! I got out of bed and walked as I had when I was a girl. The specialist let me go home. That walk has been a blessing many times in my life and I will never lose it.

Now this story has a pleasant twist to it that did not take place for approximately 30 years later in Brisbane. I was out with my husband, Eberhard and two other people we knew at the German Club in East Brisbane when a nice-looking woman approached our table. She said, 'Excuse me, but is your name Mary. Did you have three or four children and were you ever in St Joseph's Hospital, Auburn, with spinal problems?' I looked at her and thought what the heck is this about. Then my mind became alert and I said yes to all of those questions. She said, 'You are exactly as you were then; I have never forgotten your kindness to me.'

She was at that time a teenager with appendicitis and very, very frightened. So from my bed I told her how not to be frightened and if she did what I said, she would be fine. Of course, she was and never forgot me. She said she even told her own children about me because I was different to anybody else she had ever met and was kind, caring and knew how to stop pain. We sat there like 'stunned mullet' listening to this young woman's memory, and her remark that I looked the same as I did lying there in that hospital bed. It was unbelievable! After that we talked for ages about it and to think a person would remember me for my kindness. What a boost to the ego that was! Bless her. Maybe she will read my book and contact me again. It would be a double thrill...

The different things that I have suffered from in my life were, I can justly say, caused by my family directly or indirectly and have most certainly affected almost every day of my life in one way or another. Stomach aches are part of my living day, caused by a never ending set of circumstances. My thoughts can be interrupted at any given moment by flashbacks. Then it's on — irritable bowels, reflux, bladder infections. It starts up and goes on and on until the thoughts slip away again. My liver was damaged by malnutrition. I suffered ear problems, removal of my uterus through cancer, bowel problems, anal problems, the list goes on. As you would be aware, it also includes issues with sexual intimacy on a massive scale.

The effect is lifelong because it influences everything you do or say, your relationships with people and even how you shop, handle your neighbours, look at families you see together, at the movies and most of all, to hear of other victims of abuse and to know of their anguish. Yet you know that it is only one case in thousands you are hearing about. That pain can come and last hour after hour many nights. I walk around the house believing that if the pain doesn't stop, I will go insane just as my mother promised.

Eberhard (my second husband) walks at my side trying to comfort me and finally when daylight comes, exhaustion takes over. We then both rest until the next time. It can last one day, one week or whenever. I remember when my husband would drive me to a hospital and we would walk around it hour, after hour, knowing that they couldn't help me except with painkilling injections or muscle relaxants, which I wouldn't take. We both knew that I my thoughts of the past were responsible and that as long as it remained trapped inside me, it would continue to haunt me in this terrible, painful way.

I first met my second husband Eberhard sometime after I separated from my first husband Lyle. Patricia made me get out of the house and gain some order of a life back. She took me to La Dolce Vita, a beautiful coffee lounge where people would drink coffee and dance. I didn't want to go but she dragged me there. During the evening a man approached our table and introduced himself as Eberhard Tinschert from Bavaria Germany, as he clicked his heels. Patricia took him aside and said that I was recovering from an abusive husband and was quite ill. Eberhard was very much a gentleman. He could see that I was shaking and put his hand out and said, "don't shake, you are safe." I said to him "I was married and don't like men and I have children." He said "Then can I be your friend, your children must be beautiful like their mother."

Eberhard worked very hard for a year to win my trust, he brought relief and some strength and another hero who taught me to eat bits of chocolate and salami and cheese! I was hungry but I couldn't eat I wanted to be sick each time. There was no way I could learn how to get food down without his help. He did not sleep with me. It was some years later that I would marry him.

Since I began writing my pains are subsiding a little and I can say, truthfully, that the attacks are few and far between. At last, a little peace is coming into my life. My story is not for sympathy or attention, it is to show the everyday effect of living after your mind and body have been abused. You hide it in your body and it can manifest itself into pain and destruction.

Another very important thing in my life was respect. I needed it and wanted it badly. It was as if I had to have the one thing that my family denied me. I have earned it now for myself by writing this book. I have at last been able to tell it the way it really was; not the way my family would have it told. Those that are dead cannot come back and say they are sorry, and those that are alive needn't bother.

I found that there are many devastating side effects from abuse, or at least there were for me. Included in these are agoraphobia and claustrophobia. Because of spending so much time in the wardrobe and the horror associated with it, I would have thought it would have been far greater than it was. I have had to live with the effects of agoraphobia for many years; it began in my early married life and, of course, was not diagnosed as such back then. 'Nerves' was how the medical profession looked at it, so you learned another set of coping rules.

Mine was always to take someone shopping with me, as even a child's hand to hold helped me. I tried to shop in a street situation instead of an indoor complex. If I had to go to an indoor complex I couldn't cross over from one side to the other, so I went the full distance around, always staying near the wall. I was afraid to let go of support and even then I would lose my balance and feel that I was falling without control. It was terrible, plus I thought I might faint and fall down, cracking my head on the ground and bleeding (my blood again).

How I hated the terror I felt. It would come on at any thought of being alone on the street or in the shops. But my world was not filled with caring people, so I taught myself to live with agoraphobia. Today there are still little signs sometimes, but on the whole it's under my control now; not the other way round.

As for my claustrophobia, that's the odd one, because as I said, I would have thought this should have been the worst one, but it's not. If I enter a building, I must look for the exit straight away — or at least see an open door or passage way. To get into a lift on my own is a little unnerving, but if it's only a short trip, I can cope. If there are a lot of people, I won't get in or if there are too many floors, I try to walk a few and ride the rest. Sometimes I would walk all the way down.

I used to act out my part of the in-control woman and that helped a lot. I could participate in many things as long as I wasn't Mary. But now I do what I have to do and cross each bridge as I come to it. So now my life has a good flavour to it. You see, I am not perfect, but neither is anyone else. I think I said that earlier, but it's worth repeating.

Through this book I hope many people gain the strength to talk about their pain. Counsellors who read it will, I hope, gather clues to help them see through the mask which victims wear and hear the crying of their hearts. I hope, too, that the people fortunate enough never to have experienced the horror and loneliness of the abused will look and not turn away, for the sake of all people.

I am more than sure that out there are children, and adults, being abused and people know about it, but are too afraid or cowardly to try in any way to help. Think carefully. If a member of your family was in danger, wouldn't you want somebody to help, or would you understand if people turned their backs on your loved one? We know the answer, so now all we have to do is act on it. Abuse may never be banished completely, but we can sure try.

It is 1993. A little child is dead. Police saw the signs of abuse. Doctors saw it; many people saw it, but still he died from being beaten to death. It is not 1937, 1938, 1939, 1940s or 1950s. It is 2016. Why do we turn away? Why isn't it time to do something?

People say that it was different in my day. There was no help then; attitudes were different and sexual matters were not spoken of. A million reasons why people like me had to suffer. Well, this smart-with-it society of today ... lots of know-alls ... how does a kid get beaten to death, slowly in front of the world today? What's your excuse now? We have mobile telephones, counsellors, safety houses, pensions and many people trained in the field of abuse. It's even posted up in bus shelters and on walls, so that society has many ways to have a matter investigated; many avenues open to save and protect children from abuse. There is no excuse.

Many times in my life people have said I was very intelligent and quick witted, but all this did was add to my confusion because if I was so smart, why did I do, or let people do, such horrific things to me? Why didn't I see what was happening and at least try to stop it?

Well, I certainly understand it better now. If you take away the human rights of a child and teach it to function on command, obey orders and believe that its purpose in life is for others, that is how it will grow up and so I did. Now I have asked this question over and over again. Why did nobody want to help a child whose nose bled profusely at school, on buses, in the street? I repeat, most times my father would belt me across the head till my nose bled or at the best times till I passed out. I think I started to wish for the 'best beatings', so that I would be knocked out. Pretty silly, eh? At least it was peaceful when you're out cold!

Violence became a way of life for me. It was like an old shoe — I wore it easy because it fitted.

But there were also non-violent things as well ... I remember things like my half-brother's attachment to my mother and the time he wrote and told her he had a job on a property outside Moss Vale. In no time at all she had packed her things, together with some for me and we went on a train to Moss Vale. When we arrived it was just dark and we had to wait for my half-brother to arrive. It was much later and we were much colder when he did arrive. She was really glad to see him. He told her about the property he worked on and where they would live. When she asked him how far out of town it was, he told her it was quite a few miles out. Then she asked how we were getting there and he replied that he had a horse and cart waiting which he had driven in to pick us up. He said the boss had loaned it to him. She went stark raving mad and screamed at him that she wasn't doing any travelling in the night for miles and miles in a bloody horse and wagon. 'So piss off', she said, 'I'm going back to the big smoke.' Boy, was she angry, so he left us there at the station and we slept in the waiting room on the seats. It was freezing and she never stopped saying what a bastard he was to want her to ride in a bloody horse drawn wagon so that he could live with her. She kept it up, saying, 'Who did he think he was?' Well, I didn't care one way or another. Things could be just as bad anywhere she was and I had no say in it. So we went back to Chullora.

My father was just happy she was back, I guess, because he didn't punch her about or anything. It just shows what she was really like — if the grass looked greener on the other side, that's where she went, but if it was not what she wanted, then God help those involved. After all, the world belonged to her, she said.

My young self is gone now forever, I know, but in its place is a woman and one who, while still in touch with pain and anger at the loss, is able to step forward without fear; without having to apologise for the past, over which there was no control. I will never know what I would have been like had these terrible things not happened and it does not serve me well to dwell on the subject. But now I do not regret who I am today. Like a child I am looking forward. Each day has special surprises for me — I guess it's called living.

I spend my time helping as many others as I can; not just victims of abuse, but people who do not understand the system. Perhaps through no fault of their own, they are confronted with issues that might overwhelm them, but all they need is a hand to hold.

We must all try to stamp out the fallacy that parents do not abuse their children. The name for a person who abuses a child is a criminal. Molestation and sexual abuse are crimes. They are not something to cover up because it is your son, your husband, your sister or any member of your family, in case it causes trouble. Just remember that it has already caused trouble. The victim must now live the rest of his or her life with the fact that it did happen. It will not go away or disappear if we pretend that it never took place. So be a truly loving, caring and responsible person. Think of the victim and you can make it stop.

Many times in this book you will see the word 'survivor'. It is my special word. I love it and every day I tell myself that is what I am. It helps me to continue.

When I was back in the time of the victim, the pain was bad and there was no one to stop it, I didn't want to struggle with death, I just wanted to drift with it. But it was not to be and I am glad that I have the chance to speak of this terrible ordeal and help others who are still locked in.

As your memories starts to come to the front of your mind and you start talking about them, all sorts of other fears step in. You don't want to feel that pain again because you fear that when the people in your life find out, they won't want any part of you. Maybe they will expect you to prove your innocence, and just about now, you would like to stop. This will happen many times until one day, with no big guns going off, no flashing lights and no fanfare of trumpets, you will notice that you don't want to stop or turn back anymore and that you really deserve the right to be treated with respect. You are a nice, and a unique person, and you are special — you are a survivor!

The most terrible part of this story is the fact that I did not fit into the pattern of the abused person who could one day and at the right moment, find the counsellor who would help me and I would live happily ever after. That is a fairy story. It doesn't work quite like that, especially for me, and I will tell you why.

Most abuse is carried out by the male although we know that many females abuse. Mothers beat and mentally abuse children and they also sexually abuse. But the majority of abuse is from the male person. I am sure that the people who are taught to be counsellors have in their training been told about the many cases of abuse from fathers, brothers, uncles, husbands, family friends and strangers. But what happens when you have the case of Mary. She was sexually abused, tortured, mentally abused, physically abused in every possible way and subjected to an immorality that, even as educated as we are today, it is almost too hard to comprehend, and this all took place at the hands of her family, but mainly at the hands of a very sadistic female, her mother.

As those who read this book will see, such trauma was almost too much to live through. When you are young the word 'Mum' is life comfort, love, security, protection. It means that if someone hurts you, Mum will fix it. If the perpetrator of acts of horror and depravity are carried out by this female person, it takes on a larger dimension of horror and confusion. For Mary it went on to mother-in-law, nuns, sister-in-law, and so-on and so-on, until the final act against her was by another female figure.

Where does that leave Mary? What type of counsellor can handle this; what type of counselling can Mary get? She can't trust men, she can't trust women and counsellors only come in one or the other forms. So in the world of lost souls she wandered until forced into the very situation she was most afraid of. There was help, but it was from the most powerful part of her horror — a female and a counsellor to boot.

But as you my reader can see through this book, that person needed to be different, and my crime counselor was different. She was able to pick up the fact that there never had been anywhere for Mary to go, because Mary was not just another victim of abuse. She was alone in every sense of the word. This was going to take all of her counselling skills plus some more and it did. Now she can cuddle and be cuddled back by Mary. This in itself is a momentous thing. The female touch no longer makes me want to vomit and I am able to be cuddled — still not so much by women, but I am on the right road, I know that even though what I saw and did will live forever.

What has changed is how I will live with it. To the victims, you have lived through hell. I know your pain, you know mine. We will, perhaps, always feel different to others and that is because we are different. We have learned pain, loneliness and despair, but we have also learned how to survive. Many people never know about survival. Well, you can tell them because each thing that happened to you made you a professional survivor — pass it on.

One of my beloved children has already told me that he will not read this book. His reason, he said, is that he does not think he could stand to read of my terror and pain. He said he was already proud of the love I gave him and so, too he was he proud of the fact that I was his mother. He could not bear to read that there was no punishment for the abusers. I hope that the other four children can read it and use it in their own lives. Maybe, in some way, my book may help to clear a thought or a question which they wanted to ask, but couldn't. Maybe it's not too late for me to show them that I really do understand about life and for them to know that this book is for all people in pain. The sad thing is that they are the inheritors of my legacy of hurt. This may even help them if they cannot understand some things about themselves, because I did not know how to deal with my feelings. I am sure my children have grown up with the same problem. I have been so angry, but I covered up and maybe they, too, are angry. This is the terrible on-going effect of abuse.

So, because of so many things, my wish through this book is to talk face to face with other survivors of abuse; to let them see my survival and let them see themselves through me.

I would also like a radio programme to be made available for people who wish to ring up anonymously to ask the things that they wouldn't normally ask, the fears and questions that keep coming back to them.

When I think about murder, I know it is a bad crime, but in

my mind there are other crimes that are just as bad even though the victim continues to appear to be alive. I wonder how many people are fortunate to have a trauma counsellor like mine? A wonderful person and counselor from the Victims of Crime organisation; a lady that shall remain unnamed for her privacy. She has been down the road and through the gates of hell with me. She has witnessed my anger at what happened to me. This wonderful lady was the one who helped me to put little notes and little bits of paper together with the things that happened to me.

This was to become in my later life this story. Call it a book if you may because I suppose that what it is, it is a book so they say I don't know for me my idea of a book is probably something all together different but I as I said I guess it is a book. I guess it's a story that had to be told because today crime is still happening some very much like mine. My counsellor has helped me to live through the withdrawal from victim to survivor. Of course, a counsellor like this is the answer to learning to live.

CHAPTER SEVEN

Reading was the greatest thing that happened to me in my life because from this I was able to rise up. I am self-educated and proud of it. My ability to learn has enabled me to be thought of as a very articulate woman and very learned in many fields.

I have been employed successfully by top Australian and American companies as well as worked in my own businesses. There are many other jobs that could have been too far out of my reach had I allowed myself to fall into illiteracy, but I had to use the one skill that my bit of schooling had taught me. It was enough to build on. So therefore, being able to read has now allowed me to write about my life and what I have learned.

Of course, you will say what have I learned? Well, I learned what pain is. I have learned how to understand people and to know how to handle a crisis. I learned how to say No. I have learned of my innocence through my mistakes and why I made so many of them; who to blame and why. I also learned that I can love myself for the good things that I have done; for the kindness that I have felt towards other people and for the strength I have had not to want to abuse my own darling children — and to love them till the last breath leaves my body.

At this moment, while writing down my memories and feelings, I am appalled at the destruction of my life which these things caused and that at 84 years of age, I am now learning how to put 'me' first and how to stop people taking control of me, using and manipulating me so that I actually believe, they are good and I am guilty of something. I was a lonely, vulnerable, submissive woman with a terrible secret and no close friends that I could trust to share it with.

How many more are there out there in the world with secrets like this and are they getting help; will they be lucky like me and survive, looking forward to the future with hope and anticipation? If what I believe is true, there are many, many more and each one needs help. They are out there — just like me — lonely, confused, hurt and angry with lots of questions, but too afraid to talk, let alone ask, and whom do they ask?

If it had been possible, there were lots of questions I would have asked, such as were they born like other people; were they real people or monsters? Where did they come from?

I didn't know my father was an English Jew until after his death. I made contact with two of his sisters and other members of his family. It was then they explained my heritage on his side. I always wanted to know if he came from monsters or not.

I found them to be beautiful people of old age who believed him to be as they were. They have been sweet and caring trying to keep contact with me, but it was too hard for me, as I could not tell these darlings just what my life had been like and what he was like.

It appears the sudden death of his own father at a very early age was too much for him, so I paid. He migrated to Australia to leave behind his pain, I think, but instead he developed a sick and cruel attitude and used this weapon only on those weaker than himself. He fell for her good looks and her charm, which she knew how to use, and together they were well matched in evil ways. When two people like this meet and unite, the Devil takes a holiday. They were his ideal replacement. I never really found out for sure if my mother was pregnant or only thought she was at the time of her marriage to my father, but she covered herself well even way back then.

Anyway, he got what he deserved. As far as I'm concerned that man was real bad. He knew how to look like a quiet and very gentle person, but I'll always remember his cold eyes. There was death in them, unfeeling and empty of love. But for her, I think he must have felt something because when my father molested me, somehow now I have a feeling he wanted to please my mother, as well as himself. From what she said later in her older age, he was more or less her slave, so maybe there is a connection.

In the last years of her life it did not appear that she was very wanted by any one member of the family — only when necessary. So she took in a male companion who did not seem to be very bright. One day I asked her why she had this type of man in her life and she said 'If I get a smart one, he can use me. If I have a dummy, I can use him.' And she did right up to the end. She used the poor retarded man. She looked after him OK, but she was the boss. He did what he was told and she did not have to be afraid of him.

Now as you can see, my life has gone on, of course, but with some consequences of fears and phobias. They were an everyday part of living for me.

I will give you another example of the fear. I remember in Brisbane I needed to have an endoscopy. Terror struck! It was terrible. I went from specialist to specialist in Wickham Terrace trying to avoid it. I was frantic with fear, unable to explain why I could not even dare to think about it and I wanted to take the risk of stomach cancer as long as nobody even mentioned putting a tube down my throat. It went on for weeks, the doctors warning me of the risk of not having it done and my mind refusing to accept this horror, or allowing it to take place willingly. Eventually a specialist suggested I go to the centre just to look and talk to the staff. I am quite sure they thought I was more than a little over-reacting, but they were able to convince me that I would not be aware of it happening to me. At last I agreed and finally the terrible event was to take place. If only I could have told them of my reasons and my terror of something going into my mouth, especially by a male.

As we were early, we drove around the area when all of a sudden my husband, without knowing it, had driven into a dead end and was turning the car around, when the strong smell of violets filled the car. I asked my son and his friend, who were sitting in the back, if one of them had violet perfume or deodorant on. They both said "No", but they could smell it, too. So could my husband. It was sickeningly strong. Then to add to this strange happening, my husband pointed up to a street sign near the door of the car. It was Valencia Street. This was the name of the street of my home as a child where it all took place, plus my mother always wore violet perfume in honour of her name, Violet Jessie. This was almost enough to send me into a silent frenzy. Was she here with me? It was all coming back, but in front of my son I wanted to show him that you have to face some things even if you are afraid, so I went ahead with it and, of course, I survived. And, of course, the very thought of any bowel examination, such as colonoscopy or such tubes, and my flesh almost falls off me in fear.

Even the thought is too much to come to terms with.

As the reader is probably aware by now, it is not all peaches and cream, meaning that there are still times in my life that are not as good as I thought they would be. I still have doubts in telling people about my life and exposing myself to the elements of human nature, especially knowing it the way I do. I have found that although most people will tell you that they care and that their heart is filled with pain for whatever wrong the world is bestowing on others, its crap. They are only caring as long as it does not involve them. That apparently is the real human nature.

Because of all this and the memories, I still sometimes suffer from intrusive images, commonly known as total recall, when I think about my parents. I think about how I really felt about them as a child. I guess it wasn't real love I had for them. It was a different kind of love — it was being abused.

Being sent to church, an abused child looking for affection, added to my confusion because if I had faith in God and prayed to Him, then God was really part of all this.

Terror — there's that word again, the word that the dictionary describes as 'great fear, troublesome person or thing', and that is so descriptive of abused people — a great fear and if you tell, what will the troublesome person do?

You know from experience that they are powerful and have caused you such a lot of pain in the past. Will it all start again? What will the punishment be this time and can you fight now? You couldn't back then. All of these thoughts rush through your mind, but all of a sudden the thoughts start turning and you start thinking about yourself. That is the hardest thing to do because you have never done that before.

In my case it was because I was always too busy with the children; they needed me; I had to go to the school, shops, dentist, doctor, sports, do the washing. You name it, you were there for everybody and you never even thought that there was a place for you. That is the magic word: thought. Never thoughts about yourself, after all who are you?

Well now you can answer that: Who are you? If you look at yourself, you will see. You're the victim, not the criminal and you are very important; you're special; have some thoughts about you and how, in little ways at first, you can look after yourself, as well as the others in your life. If you learn to love yourself, as much as you love your children, husband, wife or whoever, then life will take on a new meaning because you will be receiving love — the special kind, the love that you deserve.

I have learned this now and the changes I see in me are terrific. I can now receive a compliment that's given to me and enjoy it, not test it. I like who I am and my character. It is kind, caring and understanding. I like that in people, too. I also like me because I tell the truth. Also the way I look and don't think about myself in any age, so over 60 doesn't mean a thing. I really mean what I say about love yourself first without vanity and that is the way to show other people that they are important, but so are you.

Once again, I will repeat myself and say the shame of this story is that a victim of abuse must learn to live with the life-long effects of it all because a criminal refuses to live with decency, self-control or respect for anybody other than themselves. We must keep our heads and look at abuse with clarity. It is a criminal offence. Why should an abuser get a short-term penalty, if any, when the victim gets life. We make excuses for them: they were drunk; they were young; it's their first offence and it goes on and on. Some of the victims were too young to be sentenced to life. It appears that the offenders get much more sympathy than the innocent victims.

It's time to stop talking about this type of crime as if it were only a minor offence. Ask the victims; look at the victims' lives and then you will have the answers.

There were many more terrible things that my mother and father did. I hope that by exposing what happened to me, you will be more aware of abuse and how it can be happening without a sound and how it affects the victims. It is a silent killer, as you can now see, and we must look closely at it, not away from it. If abusers get to know that everybody is looking, they won't be so eager to do it because their chances of getting away with it will be less.

So you see, very simply we can help prevent abuse and learn to bring this terrible crime to a stop. We can and must try — and remember, abuse is not always in physical ways. It can be the person who is yelling at the kid all the time or the person who tells another that they're stupid or an idiot. It sounds simple doesn't it? Well, it can start that way, but now that you, the reader, know about it, you have to share the responsibility of trying to prevent it. Don't turn your back.

I will give you an example of turning your back. About four years ago I went down the street where I lived as a child when I saw an old lady whom I remembered lived there in my time. She was walking so I pulled up next to her in my car and without getting out of the car, I said 'Hullo, Mrs Brown.' She looked in the car and said, 'Hullo, its Mary Goodfield, isn't it?' I was stunned at her memory. Then she said 'I thought you would be dead, I didn't think you'd make it.' I was looking at a woman who knew what was going on in my home and what was happening to me back then when I was a child. It made me angry because it was true, people did know, but did nothing. What could I say now to a very old lady, except goodbye, forever. There is a lot more I could write about sexual abuse, but the law in Australia won't allow it.

There's a certain amount of distrust in my feelings about counsellors, except for my own. She is different, and I think it's because, perhaps, she has felt pain herself. If somebody is in extreme pain inside, I believe it takes another person who has also felt deep pain to be able to help.

Of course, not all people are the same. Thank goodness! But for me, I know what works and what doesn't. Most victims of crime need something special, and each one is different. The crime of rape of one person can be equal to the crime of murder. Only a good counsellor will be able to detect the difference.

I will try to give the reader a little insight into some of the feelings that victims have. The feelings of despair are so strong sometimes that even though you have never really wanted to leave your family or whoever, the thought of death does appeal because we all have this belief that peace must follow it. After all, if it's so bad being alive, it just has to be better being dead. Thank goodness I never did it, then I would have been born and died without experiencing living. That would have been a waste.

I can remember many times wanting to go insane. This image appealed to me greatly, the thought that I could then go through life not feeling anything and not having to talk to people or having to think of things, just breathing and filling in time. Not having to say sorry; not having to like or dislike things. Just nothing, that's what I wanted. Just to be nothing and not to take up space.

The good side of my life was the fact that even though I went to extremes not to be like my parents in any way, I did not turn to substances for support. Nor did I become the prostitute, which I was unjustly called many times, or behave in an immoral way. Many times as an adult, I have wished that I could kill the ones that poisoned my childhood. This desire made me think that I would have the right to do it, but my intelligence was intact and it was only a murderous thought, never an action.

Today my thoughts are very much in order, even though I still wish for these people to be punished. I have a strong feeling of success, because here is the little girl who hardly had any proper schooling and to this day, still has difficulties doing sums. However, I did rise above the abuse. I used the skills that were still living inside me and I write my story so that others may learn from me that there is a future, and share the pain and feel the gain. Flashbacks will be around for a while, I know.

I remember while working in the prison system for the Department of Corrective Services, I always had the feeling of being able to understand a lot of the pain, self-destruction and confusion that these people were going through. I guess I saw a little of myself in most of them. I certainly saw victims of abuse with nowhere to go but down.

People with no self-esteem are easy pickings for pimps, drug pushers and clever manipulators of human flesh. They look for pain relief in drugs, drink and the comradeship of crime. Who else wants to speak with them or try to reach out to them? Not many, I can tell you from my own experience. It's much easier to criticise someone than to try to help them. More so, if they don't look the way we want them to look.

Remember what I said at the beginning of the book: "People do judge books and others by the covers they wear." I would like people to remember that the person who has tattoos only has ink on his skin; not in his soul. And the one with the bare feet walks on the same earth as you. Look for the pain; not the stain.

In my day you didn't accept women who had babies without the fathers. Today we do, no matter how many babies they have, and we teach the children to accept all mankind regardless of colour or creed. Do not discriminate, we say, unless, of course, they live next door or they have been in prison, or haven't got the clothes to shine in, or have long hair, or tattoos, or whatever doesn't suit us. Isn't it sick?

Well, at least my rotten life taught me something, and that is, compassion for those people who are the same as me. They eat, sleep and feel just like me and now, may I be so rude as to say, just like you. Of course, sometimes the abused person is suffering without realising why. They have many varied problems with their life, but because of the inbuilt defence mechanism of our minds, they have blocked out the pain and shock off the actual abuse itself, but the effects are destructive.

Sometimes, while writing my story, I have asked myself who would I rather be — the person who does not remember, for reasons too painful, or the person who does remember and then must relive and learn to cope with it? I think, without hesitation, I would say, relive and learn to cope, but that is because I have come this far. Earlier in my recovery therapy, I would have said no to going back into it. There was already enough pain in my life.

Why stir up more? Of course at that time I was not aware that I could be helped. After all, I was then in my fifties and had not heard of older victims getting any help — or for that matter, I had not heard of older victims at all. I guess it was because people think if you've lived this long, you must be OK and that maybe it didn't happen in my day, or maybe it was a problem that only started since television, dirty movies, drugs, or that today's young people ask for it if they don't wear modest clothing and cover themselves up like the olden days. But it's all wrong.

I am now in my eighties and there are still plenty of painful days, though fewer than before. So despite this, I thank myself for having the guts to go on.

I am still remembering things. I guess it's because I have lived so long and felt so much. As I remember, I will take you back in time with me, even if it is not in the order that most book readers would like, or are used to.

One minute I think I am in control, but then I discover that I am, like for instance when I was a child, trying to please at any cost;

afraid of consequences if I don't.

Shit, I hope that I can live up to what I expect of me now. I cannot slip back. At this point I am a victim again. This is every victim's nightmare that normally we won't talk about; the horror of going back. I will talk about it because people will learn if I do. My stomach is churning; I want to run; I want to be back in the closet. If I was back there, there was no choice. Whatever happened, happened. It was a way of life, but now I have to say no and it's so hard. I feel that I will never be able to.

Today, as well as all these last few weeks, I felt I had survived, but all of a sudden I am the victim. Perhaps tomorrow I will be in the shoes of a survivor again; I sure hope so.

This is my life. My life to live at last the way I want to. I will continue to survive. My counsellor is working with me. We have been through the Gates of Hell together. I know she is one hell of a smart lady and she has always said it won't be easy. I am lucky to have only hours of panic instead of the days I used to have. Dear friend, hold my hand. I am scared. Poor Mary.

I am still having trouble setting boundaries and balancing my family needs against my own. I am also having trouble setting limits with the family. I wish to stay in control. It would be easy not to, but I have decided to live. It takes courage, survivors have courage.

There was something else that really had me confused for most of my life. That was, why I continued to show no real signs of pain or sorrow, even as an adult when giving birth to my first child, my daughter. Dr Gibbons used the same trick on me as others, I guess. When the baby's head did not move, he used the knife and, in my mind right or wrong, he opened up the same place as my mother had stitched. It did hurt and in my throat I moaned or made a sound of pain. He then whacked my foot and said "we'll have none of that nonsense." Full stop. All that was missing was the bread in my mouth. He was not my father, but he also said "shut up, don't make a sound." So it was to be forever with me and that is what happened — four more children and each time nurses, sisters, saying "we've never had a patient as good as Mary. She doesn't make a sound, Wow."

Then I had a collapsed lung. Anyone who's had one will know just what I mean and mine was totally collapsed. The doctors told my husband to walk in the grounds and he would hear me from there when the tube was put in. My husband told them this would not happen, but the doctor said they did lots of big strong footballers there and they all yelled. My husband came into the theatre with me because if I was not going to be put to sleep, why not? The doctors agreed. Penrith Hospital took human factors into consideration. My husband was right, not a sound did I make, much to the doctors' surprise. But not ours.

Many of these incidents occurred in my life and I showed no sign of pain or made a sound. I had been taught well, but now through my counsellor, I can cry and if something hurts I can show it.

I can feel it because after all, I am human, have feelings. It's so different and it's so good now. I don't have to be silent anymore. I have learned that it is OK to admit to pain. I have also learned that it is OK to cry and say I am hurt, but I am still learning to trust. That is very hard. I still carry resentment at having to go back through life to live, a right that should have been naturally mine.

I remember most of the times when I must have been hurting a lot. I just left me there and waited until it ended. Then I would softly return and prepare for the next lot.

It is very much the same as the later part of my life in that I am always prepared for something to happen. And now as I look at Mary, the child in turmoil, I see that my survival is important, so that with all these things filed in their right order now and the knowledge that I have put the guilt in its place, I can help those who also want to live free of the guilt pressed on them by abusers.

Thank goodness I can now have feelings like everybody else. Each thing I did in my life was double trouble to me because I would have to pretend to be like others or I was different to the extreme. You know what I mean — no pain, no tears, just distrust of the world. So I would act a part. It helped me to come through life with my sanity intact.

To give you an example of how well it worked for me, I still wanted to be a dancer right up into my later life, but without ever going again to a dance class. It would appear to be an impossible wish until I was told of the opera Carmen going into rehearsal and that they were looking for actors, singers, dancers and Spanish-looking, of course.

So I went knowing I was not trained in any of these fields, even though I felt I could be one of the people they were looking for. When I arrived at the ABC Lower Forbes Street building, I found not one or two people there to try out for a part, but long queues of beautiful dark-haired dancers. I was definitely the oldest. Thirty-five or 36 was my age and theirs 16 to 25, I would guess, and obviously trained dancers. Well I didn't stand a chance on looks alone, so this was to be my chance to use my ability to put on a front to survive, and the money, if I got the job, would help buy a home for my children. That was the only push I needed. I walked past the dancers into a room with some people sitting at a desk. They looked up at me with expressions that said a million words! These were beautiful people and a man among them asked, "what can we do for you?" I later found out that it was Peter Weir, the producer. I said; "you want a Spanish dancer? Then look no further. I am who you want." They looked at each other in disbelief and then asked me to turn around once or twice. Peter Weir had a bit of a grin on his face. They said something among themselves and then signed me up to play the part of Manuelita, Carmen's rival.

What an unbelievable thing to happen, but it did. I played the part. It was a successful television opera and from then on I was a dancer and even today, I am still proud to say that this is a very big thing in my life. Dancing is as natural to me as breathing in and out, and without vanity I say this. I realise I played the part of the dancer and really lived it. Anything was better than being Mary with all that pain locked inside, but even now that the pain and

horror have been confronted and I have grown, I am still a dancer.

In life people do look at you and you know everyone used to say well we certainly know you're Spanish, you look Spanish. I would just nod my head, I didn't say I wasn't and as a dancer that was very good because I was in the beautiful world of Flamenco dancing which I loved.

I believe that as an abused person you can use many ways to cope and protect yourself against having to tell. It's fine to use any of your own resources to help you get through life, especially if you do not hurt anybody, but I also know that there comes a time when you have to be able to use the other resources that are available to the public and don't drain yourself. It is a terrible feeling and it's not necessary all the time; only until you learn to reach out. I wish I had been able to do these things years ago. It would have been great because when I look at things now, I can see that I would have lived better.

I guess that I really wanted to come out of the closet a long time ago, because back about 1978-79 I tried to write a story about myself, and my made-up family. I say 'made-up' because no victim ever easily admits to the world that they were abused and the worse it was, the less chance of admitting it.

If you listen to children one will say 'My mummy bought me a new dress,' and so the next child will say 'My mummy bought me two new dresses.' Every child wants to fit in and you only do that if you're the same as the others. Children want to fit into the system. Because of that I tried to write a story of my life on the road in the wagon like gypsies. Of course, I wanted to tell everything, but it was not possible. I wasn't ready to face it and it flopped. Actually it never really got started.

I thought it was better to touch wallets than to be a whore and I never wanted to be either one you know. I was lucky I guess but I always remembered my mother saying "young flesh will always be wanted."

People in power could buy anything they wanted and it was mostly powerful people that bought children, people who were not in a position perhaps to get caught or punished for what they did. It's funny, I never kept tabs on it but there is only a handful of names that I've heard of that got caught and you got to remember when I first wrote my story in early 1990's people didn't talk about sexual abuse, physical abuse or almost anything like that.

I remember so many things that were kept quiet in many ways but as you can see I'm not prepared to keep quiet and wasn't prepared to alter my story to please people who felt that they were being embarrassed or tested by some of things that I said. At the same time everybody wanted the truth but a true story is just that; based on the truth.

There's the situation where people think "oh gee you shouldn't of said that or your mustn't say that" so what do people really want? The truth or not? Should we keep it in the cupboard like we did for so many years any how it was one of those things I told the truth.

Now I am a survivor and even though I think it's not necessary, I would like it known that my marriage to Eberhard was not always easy. After all he was a man who saw things in black and white only and had to learn to live with shades of grey. He watched my pain and tried to ease me through it. We held hands in silence many times with no words that could help me. When my nights were long and there was no sleep, he was there. It was a very hard road for us, but we believed that tomorrow would be better. He loved our children and has always been there for each of them, even though I never had his babies.

Cancer beat me, but these were his children in his heart and soul. I believe they loved him the same way, I hope so.

He deserved to be loved; he earned it and you know the sad fact about everything is that so many people paid for one family's perverted minds. What a legacy! Each day has been lived twice.

My mother Violet Jessie Goodfield. A strange thing happened in this photo where my father and another image are visible

My mother never said much about her childhood but she did make mention at one point of having being saved by a woman she called a 'maiden aunt'. She said this maiden aunt moved her to live with her in a house at Kogarah. The terrace type house had a second story and a long railing along the veranda. My mother said she wanted to be in the circus and would try to walk along the railing and her maiden aunt would go crook at her.

She later told me later in her life that she hated men. This conversation started when I was looking after her in about 1969

— three years after the death of my father — when I asked her straight out if he was really my father because I was so tall and he was average height. I guess the answer surprised me after what I had seen in my life. She said she never wanted boy babies and hated even nursing them. That was one of the reasons she gave Patrick and John away in her younger life.

She told me that only the twins and I belonged to my father. The black-haired one was a ring in. She said his father was a violinist who worked in Sydney. I laughed because for the first time she told me something like a secret and only my husband and I knew, so I suppose that was a rare look at her.

She confused me in many ways, a woman who tortured her only little girl, confessing to hating men as well as her own boys.

Round about the time she told me of her hatred for the boys, she told me also that we had moved from East Sydney because my father was afraid of the people she knew there and that he would lose her to the way of life she liked best. It was getting too hot for him. He was a weak man, she said, and had no courage to face it. The house I was born in was just a few paces from Palmer Street, the heart of the Red Light district and her friends (and enemies.)

It's a pity she waited so long to tell me these things.

Maybe she wanted me to understand, who knows, but it did not help me much. I did not ever have a family. I can see that now, but back then it would have been nice.

In the years of my life I never made contact with the rest of the family. There was no necessity. First, what the family had done to me was unforgivable; second, it had left me with this terrible fear of what they could do. I had, first hand, seen the cruelty and deceit of them — I personally had been a victim of their abuse — but their vindictiveness extended right through my life. I guess it was their fear of what I knew and the fear that if they were to take the pressure off me, or their dominance, I might talk. After all, they did have sexual intercourse with me; they did mentally and physically abuse me. Even if they prefer that people do not believe this, it is a fact. I did confront them, but to get to the proof of their fear of me, they went to the extent of accusing me — and the matron of a nursing home — of neglect against my mother when she was admitted there by her doctor. She was by this time in her seventies and very much alone. I would clean her, nurse her and take tender care of her when the rest of the family said they could not, because even then I wanted her to love me and she lived in my home.

I did not ever think that my abusers were still trying to destroy my name and/or character. Because their brutality, and that of my parents, had taken away any cruelty or violence that I might normally have had — and that was their biggest mistake — I could not be cruel to anybody, especially my mother. I still wanted her to love me, I was her slave.

My nature was submissive and caring, which was why I have spent most of my life in caring type work. I had more than enough violence in my life, so, of course, all their accusations were proven false and unfounded by the State Hospital, Lidcombe. They were then given a chance to do as much for my mother as I had done. I can still hear their feeble excuses in my mind today.

But I have jumped my story again, so I had better take you back to the year of 1966 and the time she was in hospital in Canberra after being critically injured in the car accident that killed my father. Even the hospital had to allow her to have whisky to drink. If not she was disruptive and destructive.

Sex and depravity, mixed with alcohol, are a very bad combination and even in old age she was still trying. But at least I was not in her clutches then and suffering the behavior of the past. It was only mental abuse she was still trying on me in a half-hearted way, but nonetheless, she kept trying.

When I introduced myself to the ward sister, she was beautiful to me, and more than a little sorry for me. I could see this, as I was well known in that hospital for my loving attention to my mother when she had been transferred there from Canberra in 1966. I had made food and took it to her each day. I was at her side at least six hours a day, as well as looking after my children, my home and suffering the effects of my then undiagnosed cancer.

I would go backwards and forwards to the hospital and keep her quiet, because she was a very noisy, disturbing patient and not popular. I remember arriving back at the hospital one day after feeding my children, when a very nice redheaded doctor stopped me on the stairs and said; "don't go up there; go home and have a break." I was afraid to go home and not see her again, but the doctor was firm and very much aware of the pressure she applied on me. He also probably saw my ill-health showing and knew the day and nights I was always there at her beck and call. He said, "Don't worry, she will live. She is like a vulture and is surviving on your flesh."

So I went home and rested a little for two days, but my mind was in turmoil. What would she do; what would she say? Well, she survived, and then I became ill. That was 1966-67.

We will go on again to 1978. My mother was in Bankstown Hospital, having suffered a major stroke. As usual I was the last to be notified. When I went to the hospital to see my mother, I found she had been there, in a bad way, since the day before, and even though my telephone number was easy to find, I was still the last one notified, as was the custom in the family.

But back to her this last time in the hospital. It was now 1978, and this time was the final curtain for this wicked woman lying there in that hospital bed. I put my hand on her foot, just a touch, and even though they said she would not respond to any stimulants, she moved her eyes under the lids. My husband saw it also. I was frozen with fear, shame, and confusion. I didn't want to bring her back, but I couldn't wish her dead. I was sure anyway she would punish me somehow. I turned to Eberhard and said she must have known her time was coming, and though she never said she was sorry or even hinted at what she had done to me, she didn't have to. I was still her slave till her death and gave her the care she never gave me.

An older member of the family had instructed the sisters on

duty that if her condition changed, he was the head of the family and the only one to be notified, but definitely not me.

Well I had been sitting in the room for many hours when a sweet sister said I should go home and rest. I told her I was afraid to because even if she died, my family had ordered the staff, as was their custom, that only they get the call, so I knew I might not be told at all. She put her hand out to me and said "I will make sure myself that you get a call from us. Please rest."

So it was in the very early hours of the morning when a sister rang me to say my mother had just died and that I was the first to be notified. When I rang the one who had given all those instructions, the only thing he said to me was "who told you? I left instructions I was the only one to be called." End of conversation and he hung up on me. However, I was not very worried about him or what he thought anymore. Some weeks before that my mother had spoken to my husband about her death and the fact that she wanted to make sure the boys and their wives did not get her beloved diamonds. She told him she had pawned them all at a pawn shop in Bankstown. He had told her she was talking nonsense, but she said no, it was not nonsense. She had not been taking her blood pressure tablets and knew that she wasn't well, but was fed up with old age and the fact that he and I were the only ones who called to see her and apart from us; although she had visits from her man friend, but he was more than a little backward.

She said she was not afraid of death, but was afraid of the vulture family she had and did not want those women to wear her diamonds. She then told my husband that the pawnshop receipts were there for me, but my husband said I wouldn't want them. I had my own and did not want anything from her. Then, on the same day she gave me a purse and told me to open it, which I did. Inside were some pawn tickets that she said were for me. She laughed and said "I am not giving them to you. I am selling them to you because you have to pay for them if you want them." I told her I didn't want them, but would pay for them. So she said "well,

114

OK, put them in my grave with me, if you don't want them. As long as those others don't get them." She then called her friend in and said "I have given Mary the pawn tickets. I feel better now." Then she gave me another little white purse that contained some pieces of jewelry and said; "you keep these as well."

I told her she was going on silly and all this talk of death, rings and stuff was sickening. Then she said "well, there's something else I can give you that, which if you're half as smart as me, will make you rich." She then told me the secret of not turning grey-haired or wrinkling prematurely and said "open a salon and the world will love you because you can show them the treatment is good and works. You will never be poor." As yet I have never thought to open a salon even though I have proof that the treatment works. I believe the secret will go to the grave with me.

I did eventually keep what my mother gave me, though only because of what I saw the morning she died. Within an hour or so of going to the hospital, we followed my brothers to my mother's house in Conway Road, Bankstown. My husband and I sat just inside the front door and watched in horror as the three of them went through her belongings in a frenzy, putting things in their pockets and bags and words such as "I will keep this; you can have that." And then the eldest of the three held up one of my mother's fur coats and said; "do you want this Mary?"

I said "no, thank you" and went to the phone down the road where I rang her solicitor and told him what was going on. He was not surprised and said to me "Mary I received a phone call from your brother yesterday. He asked me where the will was." I was very shocked and asked him if Mrs Goodfield was dead. He said "no, she's in the hospital", so I told him to 'piss off and at least wait for her to die." I am not surprised at the behaviour; your mother was right — vultures was what it looked like.'

After my mother died I decided that yes, I would do what I felt was right and what she wanted also. I went to the pawnshop and paid for the jewellery and thought about what she had said about not wanting anyone else to get any more of it. She told my husband and I, that she had done it this way on purpose. So I put some costume jewellery in the grave with her and wore the ones she wanted me to. At least she got her wishes. My older half-brother kept saying to me "Mother was very wealthy you know Mary." I just listened and he kept repeating this on the day of her funeral, over and over.

Thanks to my eldest daughter, I was able to treat the whole issue as a joke. She was so supportive of me and because she is very sharp and intelligent, she was aware that I was being pumped for information. So when my half brother kept telling me how much he loved mother and how wealthy she was, when the priest gave me the crucifix from the coffin, I said 'If you loved her so much, have the cross, I don't want it.' She made me wear it for years. I also did not want her money, so as much as it was, I never to this day touched it, and to the best of my knowledge, no one else has either, because she made sure they couldn't. She was very cunning and had said she didn't think that they would be smart enough. It looks like she was right.

After the death of my mother, I visited my half-brother because I tried for a long time to tell myself that my half-brother was family. So with my husband, I visited him at his home in Melbourne. Of course, it was a disaster each time because in front of me, he would tell my husband I was lucky to get him and would spend hours telling me what a wonderful mother and father I had, as if to convince himself this was true. I never contradicted him or defended myself. It was not possible, but inwardly I hated him for it and wanted to tell him many times to shut up talking lies and bullshit just to make me look as if I was some sort of animal and he a saint.

Well, the end came on Christmas Day. I had my children and grandchildren at my home and was feeling so happy that I decided to ring him for Christmas. He said 'Hullo', and then 'How is what's his name and are you still with him?', referring to my husband of

20-odd years, plus a courtship of 10 years —a cruel and tasteless remark. Then he went on, as usual, to tell me how lucky I was to get a man like that and what a wonderful mother I had; she was a special lady; how much my father loved me and the life I had was wonderful.

I listened to this bullshit as long as I could; then I could take no more of his brainwashing. I hung up and made up my mind that I would take it no longer; that never again would somebody tell me the pain I suffered was not there and I was having a good time, when I was not. It would come to an end now because I was going to take control of me and not be afraid to speak out. So I have done, and I promise you I will never allow somebody to own me again.

This phone call took place the first Christmas after I'd been attacked by the woman with the letter-opener, so I guess it was all just too much.

I remember at around 20 years of age being so confused with life and my marriage, and the cruel family I had become part of, because it was different to my previous life and family. However, at the same time it was based on the same principles. I was treated as of no worth and to the people around me I was the uneducated one. As they said, I didn't even write nicely like them. They had nice handwriting. So when there were visitors, the story was told of my lack of school skills. I was just a conversational point and my pain was of no concern of theirs, even though stealing, abuse and other crimes were there. It was kept under wraps, in the guise of Christmas hymn singing.

It was then that a fine doctor started to guess that there were things happening which I was not talking about. This doctor even went as far as to say: 'If you tell me, I will be able to make sure that the culprit gets at least six months' jail.' This was the chance of a lifetime, but I was afraid of Lyall's mother. I remember she had told me once that she would commit perjury for her children and anybody who hurt them would be in big trouble. So even though

Joyce, Lyall's sister, encouraged me to do it when I told her, the fear of talking out was stronger.

This was a wonderful lady doctor, the first woman to offer to help me, not to hurt me.

CHAPTER EIGHT

There was another time when I was too ashamed to go back to the lady doctor with the problems I had, as I thought she would think me mad for not taking up her offer. So I went to another doctor who knew me, but not so well. This doctor also saw things that were wrong and even suggested so, but I kept my silence. He also told me to buy a packet of cigarettes, learn to smoke and learn to have a drink. That would help me to relax and not worry about my life so much. He said men were able to cope better than women and didn't make a fuss about things like us weak women!

So as you see, there were no avenues open like today. Nowadays he would have been in jail.

Life went on, and many sad and odd things happened. People who saw my need for love used me. After many years, the mother-in-law who wanted to destroy the love of my child for me and take away the one thing I loved so much, and who worked so hard at being cruel to me, was to benefit from my kindness later in my life, long after I had remarried. She would speak to me on the phone and tell me she had no money because the family kept using hers and how she looked after the lot and needed my help. So I would give her money, until her daughter told me it was untrue. The old lady knew she could use my kindness and inability to say no. It sounds crazy, but it's true, and my husband thought I was quite mad to give her money, and thought the woman who had referred to my lovely baby boys as 'black bastards' was using my money that

I gave so willingly, but he let me because he was being kind to me.

What a horrible way for me to realise how bad she really was and how much I needed help. But at that time I was not ready and, perhaps, like all victims, I might never have been, unless another trauma happened that would force the mind and the body to take no more.

In my case, it was one more act of violence against me that triggered the beginning of my freedom from being locked in the closet. Victims are always trying to make things right — anything to please — anything to keep the peace. I could laugh till I cried at the stories I have told to cover the pain. Even today I find myself wanting to justify other people's cruel actions. I start to apologise for them or say it was my fault. Then I pull myself up and look at what I was going to do. I was going to slip back to being the victim.

Another thing I believe is that there is nothing worse, for people who have been abused than the counsellor who tries to make out that they are in tune with the feelings of the person they are trying to help. It comes over as very weak and can lose the person who needs the help.

Once you have been the victim of abuse, you look for weakness in people and it doesn't take you long to find it, if it's there. You need the truth and the knowledge that your counsellor has been able to come to terms with their own traumas and, therefore, they won't have to pretend to you that they know and understand yours, because they will really be able to take steps with you. It will show, and because we have become super sensitive, we will see it and then we can start to trust, not before.

I guess it's a bit like being very poor and then a very rich person tells you money is not important. How the hell do they know what it feels like being poor, if they've never been hungry!

We must also realise, of course, that we do have some people who would like to help us now and who acquired their academic training to do just that and who also know about abuse. So I suppose it's up to us to try everything and along the way we will find ourselves. After all, just because a person knows how to do something, doesn't mean they will do it well. I have met doctors who have had the same patients for years and don't know them.

So it proves that you can train to be anything you want, but it doesn't mean that you are good at it. I can't count the number of times I went to a doctor for help, but the doctor wasn't looking or hearing so it just went inside and made you sick — how many tummy aches, headaches, bowel troubles and panic attacks did you have? And so the list goes on. I must say I suffered all of the things I mentioned, plus some more, but today there are many avenues that you can travel on.

Do not take the blame; you didn't do it to yourself. Try to tell; ring a centre for help even if you believe you won't be able to talk. Ring the number or write it down, go any way it comes out ... go to the police, ask for a counsellor ... ring Victims of Crime. Then if you can't do any of these things, ask yourself why and pick up the phone again. Remember, you're very strong; you're a survivor; love yourself for your beautiful strength and the will you have shown to live through things that most people couldn't begin to handle.

Survivors are special people! They take on all manner of guises to pull through each day. They cultivate acting skills and identities to protect themselves from prying eyes. They don't want to be different. To show people that everything is alright, this is the way it's done.

Never be yourself, that's too painful. I say this not because everybody is really the same — that's not so — but there are some things that seem to form a pattern and I found with myself it was easy to live in this way as against living with the pain of my real self.

I saw a TV programme on an abused woman who had developed multiple personalities, and the psychologist had said it was not uncommon for this to happen.

Well, I had visions of me with this problem because I was able to appear as an intelligent and articulate woman, very much in control and able to hold jobs of importance, plus take charge of a crisis if it occurred. Then at home and when I was alone, I'd fall apart. My fears would rise up; my mind would flash back and then the pains would start, in my stomach, bowel, or chest, and sometimes it was so bad, I would need medical help. I thought, surely I must have at least two personalities, and so the worry was there. What would I do now?

I was convinced that was my problem, and all those people who said I was intelligent must only have seen the other one of me. Gosh, now I was in more trouble, I thought. But, of course, it was not correct. Apart from the programme being misleading, my self-diagnosis was incorrect, even my trauma counsellor had to smile when I told her of my concern, and explained to me about my survival techniques and ability from within to be able to shut out the past for periods of time, and function as was necessary without pain or fear, so it was a very good way to survive.

A word of advice — please don't start to compare yourself with other people. Remember, we are all different, even though our backgrounds are based on abuse, in one form or another.

This was not meant to be a story that was to have a happy ending. When I feel that I can open more wounds that are of interest and assistance to other survivors, I will show that later in my life I was to be confronted with more tragedy and pain, such as the reunion with my baby girl thirty-five years later, the tragedy surrounding my sons and the confrontation of my other abusers, plus the effect that these things had on my life as a mother and grandmother.

I am quite sure that it will be another ladder for victims to climb to survival and, perhaps, a workbook for counsellors. I am not reluctant to talk about it because of its importance to other people, but at the same time, I don't want to feel that I have again been intruded upon and used for the purpose of self-gain for people who prey on others. I never want to be seduced by people again, and when I look back through the years when I so willingly had my children, I can see that I was seduced then by the fathers of these children, without any resistance from me at all, as resistance was not a word I knew or would have understood. Why would I want to when, after all, to be wanted was my goal in life.

These men were a good example of the people I spoke of earlier who prey on others for their own gain. I believe that it must have been more than obvious to people that I was not, at that time, skilled in life, other than submissiveness — and I can see that I was easy pickings for a person who had no character or consideration for others.

I will stop flashing back for a while now, so that the reader can have a chance to see that though the end of my book is approaching, it is not the end of my wretched story. It goes on, and the lifelong payments for my survival are high. If I get the courage to write again, I will tell you just what a high price I paid for my family's sins against me.

As you know by now from reading my book, I have lived with and understand the meaning of pain, but for me the worst was yet to come, and as I am now out of my protective world of silence, each day has to be faced ... each pain allowed to be felt. I vainly believed that I had suffered enough and did not need more. There are still so many things I don't understand and, perhaps, in this life I never will.

And the hurt is with me. Still today I wish they had loved me sometimes. I am 84 years old, yet sometimes I am a little girl and sometimes I am 113 years old. I guess this is the way it will be forever. And one thing for sure is that I will stand up and take the blame for anything I have knowingly and deliberately done wrong. But I will never again take the blame for things I did not willingly do wrong, nor allow people to run or ruin the remainder of my life.

There are many more things that I have not touched on yet. I refer to myself as Mary, and rightly so, because that is the name I was given and was known as until I was in my thirtieth year, when I met my present husband. As he was from Europe, he said that in his country Mary is known as Maria and that he would rather call me

Maria, but it was up to me. Well, I loved it. I was no longer poor little Mary, I was being born again and it was just what I needed — a new name and a new start; so for over fifty years now I have been known as Maria.

But the little girl was Mary. She has earned the right for her story to be told the way it really was. No cover ups, no little white lies to save some embarrassment. It's the truth and must be told just the way it was. She, my poor young self, does deserve to have her story told in facts and in name. This was me; this was my name and this was my pain. Next time you want to complain about your own mother, think first — did she do any of these abusive or violent things to you? If not, then get off your high horse, take your dark chipped glasses off and see another human being like yourself full of mistakes and love.

The only time Mary felt loved was when her mother used her as a pincushion. When she sewed she would thread fine little needles, make me put my hands out in front of me and put the needles under my fingernails. After she had finished sewing, she would say that I was the best pincushion she had. I had made her happy. She loved me for that. I felt no pain even though I did at one time lose my nails because of the infection I got. I was happy to please my mother.

Try to understand there is a difference between very ordinary mistakes and imperfections. We can make a lot of mistakes just trying too hard to make things right, and everybody has done that, I am sure. So look at yourself. Who are you? Are you perfect? Don't you ever say the wrong things? If your answer is truthful, you will see that you are just normal and most people are. So reach out now to loving parents because there is no second time round to have another go at it. They're here only once in your life. It must be wonderful to have the love of parents.

You will see that I have included some photos; the front cover is my mother and myself, taken just near the wine bar at Central Station, and, of course, the little grey suitcase that I told you about;

the one that she took with her everywhere so that she could carry the wine without people knowing. You will also read two copies of the letters of confrontation, that I sent to my abusers in 1991 — no replies, of course.

As well as all these photos and things, there is also a photo of Brockfields, the house where most of my torture took place and that front room — the one with the wardrobe in it — sticks out a mile to me, of course. That's the window I would climb out of in the night, dropping to the ground and then running away. The house was taken away to another place, almost as if the people knew its history. I am glad they did that because it was not a happy house and I believe that anyone else with a heart who lived there would have heard my silent screams and felt my pain. It would have driven out normal kind people. The horror was too deep. The Devil had lived there. There was blood and pain in that house which could never be scrubbed off.

The house of horrors in Chullora

Letters I sent to two of my abusers in 1991, letters submitted on my behalf by Victims of Crime.

Letter 1

This letter is in triplicate as it should be. After all, you three committed the same crimes and injustices upon me. Over the years I have often wondered what you reaction is when you see news items about incest and/or the cruelty inflicted on little girls by brothers, families and such. Do you cringe inside like me, or do you pretend that you do not approve, or even say that you could never understand anybody doing such terrible things to a child, or maybe going so far as to say you would kill anybody who touched your child? Well I have said all these things and meant it, because as you will remember, I am one of those little girls. You sexually abused me. I hope you have all treated your own children far better than you treated me. I hope you never sexually abused them or physically and mentally destroyed them.

I have lived with the terrible memories of this abuse and tried to forgive you all for blackening my heart and my spirit, but I never could. You also blackened my name so that I thought no-one would listen to me. Well, I'm out of the closet now and it's a fact that each of you did sexually, physically and mentally abuse me.

You once said in front of your wife and children that you would not sleep in the same church as me. Well, now you can tell them why – what you ***** and **** used to do with me. No wonder going into a church would have been a bit much even for someone like you, or are you going to suffer a loss of memory now, or try to declare me *mad or a liar or whatever. Well, it doesn't matter what you say. I now fully understand your methods and why you did what you did. I suggest you now face up to what you did.*

You said I was a very bad woman (slut was the name you used to that Fairfield Policeman.) So what does that make your apart from a slanderer?

So now you can all tell your families why it's so difficult for you to look me in the eye. I am not a little girl now, but my memory is very good. How's yours? Your families can read this if you let them. Get ready to explain, all this dirty stuff to your family. You were always pretty good at telling stories, or at least up till when your mother died, and I am sure you will do your best to make this sound like a nasty lie that Mary is making up. But it is not. Perhaps in your church it is called something else, but in mine its called incest.

Thanks to society today, I am able to write this letter to you and not feel guilty, nor hide it away any longer as you have all done. I believe it's time for all of you to come out of hiding and face up to what you did. You all had loud voices for so many years, so loud that you drowned me out, but I have found the voice and the strength to see you for what you really are, not for what you say you are.

May God forgive you, I never will.

Mary Goodfield

Letter 2

When talking to you on Xmas day I found you talking like a stupid old man to me, such things as what a good home life I had, and what a good father I had. That my mother was the greatest women there was, and how you hope to meet her again when you die.

Well I hope so too because it will be in hell. You did not know or care how I was raised, you were always on the run from the police or in jail and you only called in to fuck my mother and I sure remember you doing it.

You and her did not care about what I saw in the side room so why do you preach to me of that wicked women you called mother. As for the rest of my childhood it was made up of Sexual abuse from your brothers and physcial abuse and cruelties. You were never their long enough to see and as for that women and your stepfather. I received the legacy of their sick physical abuse on record at the children's hospital Camperdown and Caterbury hospital.

But you would not want to know about all this, I am sure its too close to the bone for you to take, well you all tried to make me look like a very bad woman so that if I looked bad enough you might all lood good. Plus no one would believe me or my story of what horrors I saw and felt at the hands of the Goodfields, but all my life I have lived with it and felt the pain every day of my life.

And still I tried to forgive you all and I thought I had done so until you said all that crap to me on the phone abut my wonderous childhood that you made up because you knew nothing about it. And to ask my husband, what would you know about a good woman or a good marriage. Your idea of a good women was a mother that you could have intercourse with, so your judgement is more than a little bit off wouldn't you say.

And now I let you and your brothers know that I am going public with all of the ugly truth so that others may beware of hidden horrors that children do not always expose no matter what happens in their sad torn little lives, and how some men can make it sound right about what they did even though it was very wrong.

And how a little girl can have her life turned upside down by people like you and your brothers and mother and step father. Well, my darling children are grown up now and know the truth and understand that it is time for me to come out of the closet and show the people of our society that there is a right time for everything even exposing people like the Goodfields and the Peels who live as if they have committed no sins. Yet cast stones at the innocent.

May God forgive you, I won't.

Mary Goodfield

PS: If you or your brothers wish to deny any of my story, feel free to do so through the judicial system, or public opinion as will be the case when it's released. I will give you all a better chance that any of you gave me after all you made people believe I was guilty of anything you all wanted to say, I had no voice until now.

If my family had asked me, or told me to commit a murder there is no doubt in my mind I would have done so, just to make them happy with me. Thank goodness they didn't ask. I don't know if I could have lived with that. It is bad enough knowing what I was made to do without anything else and murder was just about the only thing I didn't do for her.

Thank goodness I survived, and I say to all survivors that if you look at yourself, you will see a person who does not need sympathy and does not need patronising, but just needs people to know so that we can be free forever. Help us to expose the guilty ones; don't let them hide behind us; don't let them lie and threaten, then get away with it. Let it be a safe world for all.

I am older now and I need every moment of time to live. My past is gone forever. Whether it was good or bad, it is no longer here and only the dark shadows remain. Broken child, healing woman is how I see myself. How you see me is not really important. You weren't there when I needed you, so don't tell me now what I should have done. Just help each other. Don't look away again. It's not your neighbour's problem; it's yours, all of you. Don't say I knew it, when it happens, because if you do, then it means you turned your back and another victim cries.

As you are no doubt aware, I have not spoken in detail of my five children or the effect of my upbringing on their lives. I have deliberately avoided this subject because I feel I must let the reader know and understand what took place in my own life by staying with this story of horror from a very early age: (1) because it should be known; (2) it has helped me by telling it and others will be helped by knowing about it; and (3) to show therapists and the system that there are older victims and that females do abuse.

If we are just getting the victims to admit to male abuse, it is also a responsibility to discuss female abuse, so that the victims need not feel like lepers. You have a chance to know me first-hand through my book, and when I write again about the further tragedies that befell me and mine, it will help you to see the whole picture and not have to put it together like a puzzle.

To this day, I love my babies, so that much didn't change, but they grew up, as I have now.

This is one of my lists of survival techniques:
- Fantasizing
- Perfectionism
- Avoiding intimacy
- Leaving my body
- Staying busy
- Taking care of others
- Not sleeping
- Humour
- Avoiding sex
- Staying super alert
- Pretending it didn't happen
- In control of thoughts (I grew up)
- Fantasize or Die

Here I write my honest opinion on the stages a victim goes through. I believe there are many stages and, in fact, too many to list. But it is my belief that there are three that I went through, so even if some people will disagree with me, this is how I saw myself and the stages.

Stage one: the crisis stage: I can't believe it ... why me ... I panicked inside ... sick vomit ... faint ... no, it didn't happen ... don't talk ... cry inside.

Stage two: the suffering stage: It did happen ... nightmares ... pain ... flashbacks ... started to work through feelings ... my suffering started to decrease.

Stage three: resolution: I can live with it ... bad self-image on the way out ... will not let myself be used ... but never forget ... I am a Survivor.

Sometimes I still get the three mixed up together, but it does not last as long as it used to, so I know its working. But I would not recommend trying to do it alone. I believe survivors of abuse have an inbuilt ability to work through more terrible traumas than other people, but there is a time, even so, when we must accept the assistance of somebody who is skilled in working with our pain, and with their help, people like myself can live better. I have improved so much that sometimes I don't believe it, and wait for the crunch, but it doesn't come. The worst I get is a 'downer' for a while; I might start to feel something is getting on top of me, instead of me being on top of it. However, after a short time I can now turn most situations around.

Look for the signs: When I was a child, how would I have identified myself in a crowded room. I was the quiet one, I was the one with the strange walk. I was the one whose nose bled all the time. I was the one who just looked, but never touched. I was the obedient one. I was the one who was always running away. I was the only child who loved the dark. I was the one who didn't compete. I was the one who always had cuts and bruises and marks. I was the one who didn't have her hair combed. I was the one who couldn't eat chocolate without vomiting. I was the one who didn't drink lemonade. I was the one who was tortured, abused, unwanted and knew it.

Later as a young woman, how did I identify myself.
I was the one who offered to carry the parcels.
I was the one who made the cups of tea while others rested.
I was the one who offered to run to the shops.
I was the one who stayed and talked to the old people.
I was the one who knew what to do if you were upset.
I was the one who offered to do all the work.
I was the one who came when you called.
I was the one who always said its OK.
I was the one they used for all odd jobs.
I was the one who was always smiling.
I was the one who was the life of the crowd.

I was the one who made all the clean funny jokes.

I was the one who picked everybody up.

I was the one who never got tired.

I was the one who was up first in the mornings.

I was the one who cleaned up and went to bed last.

I was the one with the cultivated sleek walk.

I was the one who put her hand over her nose.

I was the one who always looked for exits in buildings.

I was the one who taught women how to have their babies without making a sound.

I was the one who gave things away to people even when I wanted them myself.

I was the one who ate last and least.

I was the one who never cried.

I was the one you turned to in trouble.

I was the one you stole from and I wouldn't say a word.

I was the one who agreed with everything that was said to me, good or bad.

I was the one who didn't defend myself, never.

I was the one who would give my abusers money when they asked for it.

When the accident happened that killed my father in 1966, one of my brothers wanted to take his teenage son on the plane that the police arranged a charter for at my request. He said he had no money for the fares, so I paid for both their plane fares out of some money that Eberhard had given me for Christmas. There was no thank you, which is normal from anyone, in return for my kindness. But later in months to come the same brother told people that I was definitely a prostitute, because when I paid the plane fares for him and his son, I had a roll of money in my purse, and no decent woman has that much money, so he didn't intend to pay it back. I did not defend myself by telling where the money came from, or calling him a disgusting creature, but just let him continue to destroy my name.

This is how you could easily identify me in a crowd. The Giver ... The Doer ... No Defence ... No Fight ... No Lies ... No Cruelty. This is how the victim is destroyed. The abuser speaks out in lies and the victim dies.

I decided to see people's reaction to abuse. To be precise, their reaction to a book about abuse. I asked two large publishers, one publicist, three middle-aged women, three middle-aged men, one male writer. All not interested ... it's been done before ... it's a terrible thing ... not enough people interested to buy a book on it. Television covers it pretty well these days. Full Stop!

The same people were told that the book has torture, murder, depraved sexual acts in it and looks like being the only one of its kind in Australia. The depraved acts mainly carried out by a depraved mother, well that makes it a different thing. It sounds very interesting and people will be more attracted to this story because of the torture and stuff. Yes, interested. Full Stop!

I believe this shows the lack of interest in sexual abuse, except for the morbid curiosity of people who have depraved behaviour, the dirty people, the ones who do it or the ones who are only interested in reading about it, but not bothered by it otherwise.

When my mother died, the family decided to put the plaque on her grave to read: MAY SHE REST IN PEACE. Well, I just could not let this happen, so with my husband, I went to the cemetery to speak to the people concerned, and had it changed. It now reads: LORD HAVE MERCY ON HER.

I felt that she didn't deserve peace after all the things she had done to me, but I could at that moment feel mercy. She died without ever loving her daughter, and there was not one person at the graveside who came as her friend. She had confessed to my husband and me that she did not feel love for anyone. So I guess she needed mercy and for her sake, I hope she got more than she gave.

I wonder how often you've felt anger and resentment, plus a range of other emotions, when you felt that somebody had not given you what you thought they should have. Well, as I looked at

her coffin, I had the feeling that this woman could not be in there. How dare she die without loving me; without telling me she was sorry. Her final act against me was that she left without telling me why. There is still anger in me, but of course, not as much, and that's good because it's a little less painful to live with.

In my book and in my life I make no apologies to my children, family or readers. The things I did in my confused and tortured young life were not of my wish, but of the wishes of the sick, ill and perverted people who used me for their own advantage. I have given love and caring attention to all I came in contact with during my life.

The only regret that I have is not knowing that I was a good woman and mother and not setting boundaries to allow my own children to grow within themselves. In my childhood I could not learn to say No, because it would have endangered my life, I'm sure, and also for fear of my parents not loving me.

I did the same with my own children. I never said No in case I lost them. Ever since, I have learned that you do not lose someone who loves you by saying No, but you may lose someone who does not respect your rights, and if you have no rights, you have no love.

As I look through this book I see pain and sorrow. It's all there, and the rotten part is that it could have been prevented. I was brought up in a world of 'Do-Gooders', but not one of them wanted to see what was in front of them, and I believe that nothing much has changed today. The same 'Do-Gooders' are here; they talk a lot and they know a lot, but they don't do much more than that. So violence and abuse goes on. I will go on also, because I am a very strong woman and there is a lot I must do. There are people in abusive and incestuous situations who will never reach out if we don't reach in.

You know, I wish that my life could have been different in so many ways, for so many reasons. The main ones I guess are for my own family. And how lovely it would have been to have memories of love and happiness and tenderness, laughter and togetherness. How I envy those that had it. What a story that would have been — a real love story. Instead I must say that there is still a lot that isn't said in the first part of my story.

One of the things missing was my true feelings about my mother, and I am sure many people would like to know what I really felt, and still feel, about her today. Well, I will tell you. When I was small and thought that each time I did what she wanted she would love me, it didn't hurt much. But as I got older and knew with my strong instincts that she didn't love me, I started to feel anger. It was not big or loud anger. It was just there in my stomach all the time and behind my eyes, sort of like tears. But I didn't cry. I just hurt all the time. It was a terrible feeling and only another survivor of this type of torture and abuse will understand the pain and anger that live inside the victim. Because there is no way to let it out — no tears, no screams, no hitting back in any shape or form, just a world of silent pain that many victims endure day after day, weeks turning into months, then years never ending, so that eventually, your mind does not belong to you and you never get prepared to live in the outside world.

This is the world you live in, and it's the only one you know about. So each day the anger sits inside you until you are no longer the little girl you were born to be. You are a confused, sick and hurting person without identity. You are the victim of abuse. You look like a little girl on the outside but inside you are older than life itself. You have felt and seen things that most people never read about and you want to scream out:

'Love me, please, and forgive me for being born. If I had known it was going to be like this I would not have taken my first breath. I know the world has mercy for babies who die — but what about mercy for some of us who don't die? And don't live either?'

That's how I felt when I was young, because I knew that the monster who dished out hell was my mother. The woman with a smile on her face and a demon in her heart was called Mum. I didn't know it was called hate back then. But now I realise that even as a little girl, my childlike love turned to hate as I learned to live in pain and fear of the worst type of abuser. The one that the prayer books say I should love - The Mother.

Now, as an adult or old lady, whichever term you want to use, how do I feel about her? That person who gave birth to me and wore the title of Mum? Well, for her sake I am glad she's dead, and for my sake, I'm sorry she's dead. I say that because if she were alive now she would be old and frail and I would be too kind to say to her all that I could. But I guess it's no good pretending that I have forgiven her. I have not, and in my heart I still hurt very much and still feel the pain behind my eyes each day of my life. I still see and hear her and still relive many of her horrific tortures. It is a constant reminder that I did have a mother, and it would have been so much better to have had none.

I am in recovery, that's for sure, because I can now truthfully say I hate her for what she did to me. But I can live with it. For some people, they must forgive to recover but that is not so for me. We are all different, and my way is best for me. As other people have theirs, so it will be. She was a monster in every way. Each breath she took was stolen from some person who really deserved it more. She lived on hate and depravity and used people only to satisfy her own needs. She never gave love to anybody, I know that for sure. Her life was made up of what was best for her and nobody else. She gave me life in one hand and destroyed it with the other.

Because of her, this book has been written. I hope that wherever she ended up they showed her the same mercy she showed me. And yes, I know I have said that earlier in my story, but it's worth repeating.

Now you may say 'that's that'. But it's not quite like that yet. You see, while ever I live and breathe, I may have times when I will need guidance to help me live. There are still rough patches but fewer and very far between nowadays, thank goodness. But when I look back to the early stages of confrontation with counselling, it's unbelievable.

I remember when it was time to see my counsellor I would try to prepare what I would say and do. I would tell myself that I was only going to talk about light and airy things. No big things, no pain today. I not going to discuss my horrors, or how I felt about those happenings in my life and nobody was going to make me — full stop. Then there I was, talking to this woman, my counsellor. And may I repeat, this woman, the enemy.

It's very strange now that I am living outside my closet and a woman showed me the way in. And a woman has shown me the way out. That is more amazing than you think when you look at it. Each day now I do not hide behind my pain but see and face life as me. It's not always great, as most people know. It sure does have its rotten moments. But at last, I am up there. Front row living and respecting myself and demanding my share of kindness as I give it out. Turning the other cheek maybe all right for some people, but not for me anymore.

Although there may be that odd occasion — after all, no one's perfect, are they? What I am really saying is that I am no longer afraid of others or myself for that matter. I know that each person has their share of mistakes. What makes things different is, were you trying to do something good when it turned out bad? Or were you just doing something bad because you wanted to hurt somebody?

There is a big difference, you know, and I know it better than most people.

It took a long time and a lot of work with the counsellor to become aware that I did not have to carry the guilt because I did not have the skills of life, as they should be taught us. If people had done more helping than condemning, a lot of changes could have been made.

We must rely heavily on trained counsellors and survivors, to see that the mistakes that were made are not repeated over and over again, or that people without the correct skills of counselling are not allowed to attend to victims, only making the matter worse. I was put in this position on more than one occasion with trained but unskilled persons who really shoved me back a hundred years. If the person you see says something you know is wrong and can't explain to you the reason, or if you are very uncomfortable with that person, your instincts are telling you it is not good, your chances of being able to talk to them are slim. You need to feel trust and be comfortable enough to tell them your innermost secrets. Do not expect them to agree with more everything you say, or that you must always be right. After all, you are reaching out for help and to do this you will need someone who can guide you with honesty, experience, and the ability to let you see yourself as maybe you have never done before, so that you can look at the skill with which you have survived already, and see the real and wonderful you. How strong you really are, what a special person you are and always have been.

The counselor you feel really comfortable with is the one that is more than likely able to walk with you through your pain. It was, and still is, a long road for me. But worth it.

Anything is better than the way it was, never defending myself, never setting limits, never able to say no. Always afraid of losing the people I cared about. It's different now even though I still hurt. I won't be buying love anymore. I have earned it with my kindness and sincerity and generosity. There is no greater love than that I have been given.

All my life I had the feeling that I was invisible. When as Little

Mary I was not spoken to, it was as if people did not see me, especially my family. I was an object, a something to use. But I was not visible to talk to. This continued on in my life as you read earlier. My rights were very limited and not obvious to me, and this went on into my adult life, where people used my kindness and my inability to say no. It was as if I was an object, not a person. Even though I had a name it felt as it I wasn't really there for them to see.

But now I am clearly visible. I'm no longer an object. I guess I see me now. It's great — at least, it is for me. You know. It was not my imagination that people treated me like an object.

I remember a very respected doctor who, as well as his normal practice, liked to run his hypnotherapy practice and of course, I thought this kind doctor might be able to help me live with my terrible secrets. So one evening my husband dropped me off there and I went through his form of hypnosis. After it was over I said I wish I could go to the doors of my abusers, or write to them and tell them how bad they made my life. The Doctor, as if he did not even see me as a person or as a victim of abuse, said, 'You wouldn't want to do that to them now at their age, would you? It would or could ruin their lives.' He did not consider my life or the destruction they had caused me for more than 50 years. I walked out of his practice with lead in my heart, I had been once again pushed back in the closet by a doctor — a man who was in a position to heal or destroy lives. How many did he crush?

I did not seek help again until my brush with the person wielding the letter-opener and my fortunate introduction to Victims of Crime, and my counsellor.

So, like I mentioned earlier, we need skilled people to help, not hinder us. It is not a job for the unskilled. After all, they can only add to our despair and give less hope for people who need hope and love and trust. And of course, that's the hardest thing of all — learning to trust. Each day now, I see examples of learning to trust. Such as when you meet people and of course, you would be foolish to trust people you have just met. But at the same time, you must learn not to judge them all as being bad like it was before. So the way it's working for me is I listen to myself and if I feel fairly comfortable with them, then I allow myself to take it STEP BY STEP. I don't trust immediately. But I don't underestimate myself. I just go easy and time will show me more about this person.

I am seeing that it is working well for me and slowly there is some good in my life. Not a lot, mind you, but it's more than it was. And I know not to believe all that is said. I take what is unsaid and mix all this with a bit of commonsense. I'm learning about living with skill and being a survivor. I knew about living everybody else's way but not how to live for me as well — or even, at all. It's different. I'll say that. What a lot of living I've missed and I sure made it possible for a lot people to live well, if you know what I mean. No worries, leave it to me, I will fix it, no money, 'have mine' — it's so terrible I could laugh at it. And let me not forget to say that I do have a good laugh sometimes. I believe it's called black humour and it is good for you. Well, it's good for me to laugh, maybe because it's so terrible — I won't even try to explain it to you. Life has taken another turn and for the best, I'm sure.

I wonder how many people who read my book will identify with parts of it in some way? And it they do, will it help them? I do hope so. Perhaps even knowing that they are not alone, because the isolation of abuse in itself is so lonely. No-one deserves to feel like that. We build dog boxes for our little dogs, and let cats sleep on the lounge. We protect our canaries and any other animals, and I agree with that. But we must also give love and care to fellow humans and look to see it they need our help.

I believe that judges must be made more answerable to the public in regard to the penalties they issue to persons who commit crimes of abuse against other persons. This includes rape, violence, sexual or mental abuse. They should indulge in learning from victims. Know more about the profound effects of these crimes and in doing so, they will be in a better position to judge and penalise. We will then have more faith in the system.

Let us not forget the offender. We must consider how this is best approached and look at and what is wrong with the way we are handling things now. Is prison itself the answer? What do we do with the abused person who becomes the abuser? Will they be judged on the amount of abuse used on a person by them, or the amount of abuse suffered from others by them? Again, were they abused? Or is it a good copout to use? Are they treatable, or not? Can people who have raped and abused be helped? Or should they just be put in jail forever, out of the way of society so they don't get the chance to do it again?

Well now you are saying, 'I don't know. Let the courts decide, because it is too hard for us anyway. It's easier if we just lock them up forever, or castrate them, or hang them. Who knows what to do, just don't let it happen again, especially to one of my loved ones.'

Isn't it a terrible thing to have to decide on? So really we must feel a little for the judge who has to decide for us. Either way, the decision can be wrong from somebody's point of view. The only thing is that we must keep our heads and don't panic or feel that you must decide a certain way or you will offend. Because I think that's one of the reasons that things have not been handled correctly. People don't really say what they believe themselves. They say what they think people want to hear and so we have groups of people making decisions to please, whether it is right or wrong, and I believe that's bad. And I am sure you will agree with me.

How did I really get through life with some of these horrors locked up inside? Well to tell you truth I tried many times to reinvent myself because I thought it would work that way, but because it wasn't true I failed. I had all sorts of stories made up of this family I wanted to pretend I had or I didn't even want to speak of.

CHAPTER NINE

You know, an odd thing just happened while I was writing. The phone rang and a person I know asked about the book. Out of the blue she said; "Maria, you never speak about your mother's background. Why?" After explaining to her as best as I could, it made me realise that the readers may be interested too. Even though it's still not really clear to me, we did a fair bit of searching, but met a lot of silence regarding her background. But I will share with you all that I found out.

First I got her birth certificate and even that had some parts crossed out on it. But armed with this piece of paper and a map, hubby and I went off in search of some answers. I think I was hoping to find reasons for the way she was and for a happy ending, or at least something like that. But it turned out to be even worse, and more hurtful and confusing than I wanted to hear.

Now of course, I will alter some names in telling you what happened because I am very sure the people in this story will not want it known, nor where they live. So the story is true but some names and places are not true. There are people who do not deserve to be hurt by their history or by me, so please try to understand what it's all about. After all, if I must tell you about my mother's background as true as I know it to be, then this is the only way I can do it.

So there we were in a country cemetery, looking for her parents' names on the headstones. Unbeknown to us, because it was such a little town, we were being watched. Strangers in the cemetery get noticed as you might guess. Well, we were getting nowhere. We found one name, but not the other. It was getting confusing. Then I saw a man and asked him did he know of the family.

He gave a bit of a grin and said "No, but go to the house just across the road apiece. The man there will help you, for sure. By the way, his name is Old Bluey."

So off we went and as we drove up the dirt road, I could see people at the gate of the house that the man had sent us to. I looked at the old man and his eyes reminded me of my mother's eyes. Brown, not quite as dark as hers, but they showed a likeness. As I walked towards him he said, "Hullo girl."

I answered, "I'm Jessie's daughter, Mary."

He put his arms around me with tears running down his weather-beaten face and said, "don't look no more girl, you've found your home." He called for the rest of the family and his wife took us to the house, crying out, "It's Jessie's girl. She's home."

My heart was beating so fast and I was sure it would stop and I would be dead. I'd thought I'd found my family and they looked happy to see me. Everybody was talking at once. It was a sight to see and hear. Then they brought out a photo of Old Bluey's father and as I looked at it, the shock went tearing through me. I looked at my husband and could see that it was not my imagination by the look on his face. You see, the photo we were looking at was the image of my eldest boy in every detail. It was a shock to say the least and my mind was spinning with questions and joy and fear. What to say? What to ask'? Where was I to start? First they knew by our expressions that the photo was a link, but then things got very confusing. I told them that my mother had said her father always wore white suits, spotless all the time and in my mind I had thought maybe my grandfather was from the tropics because I thought that up there they wore white suits in the heat.

Then Bluey's wife said that his father wore a lot of white because he played cricket and wore it even for the photo. So things looked as if this man in the photo was my grandfather, and Bluey was my mother's brother — my uncle. And he had another brother.

But then things got topsy-turvy — his father was married to his mother all right, and she was a white lady, but he had no sisters, such as my mother and her sister, Mary. And nobody could fit them in except for the naked truth that his wife remembered. That was that my grandfather was a respectable married white man, who had sexual encounters with a black woman (Aborigine) with only one name. She was called Jess and lived in the bush. When two little girls were born they were half white, half black and unwanted. But it got more confusing because he gave my mother his name, but that's all. Yes, his name was the name my mother told me he had. And he did wear white clothes a lot of the time. So everything was right — this was my grandfather. No doubt in anyone's mind.

But my grandmother was not the lady on the birth certificate. All the evidence supports the fact that my Nana was Jess the Aborigine, and my mother was Violet Jessie. I cannot find any more evidence one way or another, so I have accepted the facts as I saw them. At least it explains my mother's looks. Dark brown eyes, jet black curly hair, broad nose, short body, soft pretty skin — and to tell you the truth, to see the rest of the family and in my own heart, the look is there in some of them. But for myself, I'm not sure. I have my father's Jewish looks, I'm told, though I was very olive-skinned when younger which seems to be fading as I age. But I am now a very proud woman if this is or was my Nana.

I am just not proud of my mother for the terrible things she did. No race, colour or creed could be proud of her or her actions. It has nothing to do with race. It was her.

Now, it sure looked really good for me then, finding out who my mother was, and my grandfather. Because even a little bit of family was better than no family at all. And of course, I was hoping that I would find out why my mother was the way she was. It did not work out that way at all. Not long after I found this family, my old Uncle Bluey disappeared. The reason, the family sadly told me, was that he was found to be sexually abusing his granddaughter, and apparently had been doing so for some time. I had just been dealt another blow to my self-esteem. I never made contact again. My family of horror was complete.

Since all of this has taken place, I have felt no need to look any further for answers among the people. The only answers I need now are from myself. It is not important where I came from, or what my colour or race is. It is important how I feel about me, the person I am, and liking who I am today.

I guess I have now touched on many important parts of my life, and it's a bit like living in a house with no blinds — at the windows I am totally exposed to the world, and to those people who will understand, and those in pain, and those who want to learn, and of course, to the others, the ones who will look at it like a bedroom window. Well, that's all right, because I have written it for all who care, I was not forced to write it. The choice was mine. I'm glad I did, and I hope others get courage from it.

As you are aware, I have five children, two daughters and three sons. I had a daughter first, then a son, then another daughter and then two more sons. Their ages range from 65 years down to 55 years and you are probably curious about them and how they grew up, and what sort of a relationship I have with them now? Well, all these questions are in the process of being answered.

I am dedicating the next of my writings to my children warts and all. It is on the way. Very interesting and very sad in parts, indeed, very human — but I have stuck to the truth again, and will let the world see, and feel, and decide whatever they want to. You see I love my children very much just as I did when they were born. But I see them differently now.

Of course, they are people not just my children and as with all people, they each have their own minds with likes and dislikes, hurts that you can see, and hurts you can't see. Of course I would wish for them to reach out and love me as I love them, but this may never be. Maybe they will wish to punish me for their lives and for telling the world about mine. That is the price survivors often pay for telling the truth. If it is to be this way, then I will have to survive

it and show others that it can be done. Because I know in my heart
that as a mother who loves and cares about her children, my greatest
wish is their wellbeing. Perhaps I also wish for an understanding of
my pain and a loving pair of arms to hold me. Yet, at the same time,
it may not be possible for my wishes to come true. Not because my
children don't care or perhaps love me enough to be understanding
of my tortured life, but because my life may have caused them to
feel the pain. Certainly not through sexual abuse, or physical abuse,
or mental abuse by me, but by my lack of knowledge of simple
living skills and the ability to defend myself in front of them. May
this story give them the strength and ability to be as they would
wish to be themselves. They have no need to be what I want but
they will always be my babies, and in my mind, my reward for
punishment I did not deserve. I do not wish to cause them any
embarrassment in their adult life. If they do not acknowledge the
name as their mothers and their relationship to me, that is their
right and I respect it.

But don't let the words fool you. Underneath those words
are hopes, fears, and a mother screaming out 'Love me as I love
you.' Those of you who have survived some form of abuse will
understand what I have said in this book. Each of us has felt loss,
pain and fear. Always remember that to love yourself is the best way
to gain peace and happiness because no one can love you more.
After all, it is up to you to set the standard. If you don't care about
yourself, nobody else has to care either, that much I am learning day
by day. But not without some pain, I warn you.

You know, when I was more than halfway through writing this
book, I felt that lots of things were going to change. And they did —
well at least, things are different for me. But nothing else has changed
much, such as people who are cruel, people who tell lies and hurt
others. These people will always be there and as a survivor I am still
very much in the beginner's stage of learning new ways to cope with
them. I really thought in my heart that by the time I got to the final
stages of my book I would be fully in control of my life and would

end the story with great tales of success, of how, after letting all the pain out of my heart, I would be free at last and that nothing would affect me. Well let me continue to be honest and tell you that my life has turned around and of course, for the better. But just when I think I'm fully in control, something happens and I'm hurting and scared and not handling it as well as I thought I would. So it's a very slow process for me and of course, I wanted it to happen quickly. I wanted to be the new me straight away, and that's not the way it is. After all, years and years of my type of living can't just go away as quickly as that. Now at least, I am not expecting instant miracles, but it is working. There will always be rotten people around but I'm coping with it all with my new skills in caring about me.

It's really strange when I say 'no' to something that I don't really want to do now — when before in my life, I would have said 'yes' and put up with it, no matter how bad it was for me. So I guess recovery is slow for people like myself and other survivors.

By the way, another experience I have had since beginning my story was accidentally involving myself with a group of people who had me believe they were Christians of a denomination I had never encountered before. I tested the water to see if things were different from when I had been subjected to Christianity in my early life. I am sorry to have to say, I found that nothing had changed. Maybe there's one real non-judgmental caring person out of 20 who are fake. You know what I mean, the sort that keep telling you they will be there for you — that is, until you need them. That's okay by me really because standing up by myself is the right way for me. Possibly not for everybody, but it's what I know best and then I can keep my expectations down to a minimum and get on with learning how to be happy in this world as it is, instead of expecting great changes from others. It is up to me now. No one will hurt me again. I will win.

Once upon a time people could make me believe that all the terrible things they did to me was my fault. Well, thank goodness I know now that they were responsible for the horror that was called childhood. For me to be terrorised for so many years is against human belief. I was worthless in my mind, so much so, that I couldn't even live in the real world like they did.

Well, here I am in my 80's and near the end of my book. The sad hurt and painful beginnings and my stepping forward still carry the scars, but I am able to help so many others to reach out and know that there is somebody like myself who is ready to understand their lonely pain and confusion.

Live on, my friends, we deserve it. Join me in proving we are strong, we are different, and we are survivors. And we still have a life to live, and a good one. Not just breathing in and out. If I can, anyone can. Speak now. I can promise you that you will be listened to.

I guess the really sad thing about my story is the fact that it is only one story. I am sure there must be many, many more people out there with a wall of pain around them who have lived in silent fear of having to tell and not being believed, or keeping it locked in their heart and mind until it's almost too much to live with.

I'm sure we are all aware by now that abuse comes in many forms and not the least is the abuse you can receive at the hands of the law, or should I say, part thereof. The police prosecutor who in his zest for winning a case, may, with the approval of the court raise his voice, glare across the courtroom at you, and declare you a liar. Treat you as a person unfit to give a truthful account of anything. Perhaps even a lover of the accused, be male or female. He stands while you must sit. He can say anything, in any tone of voice, but you cannot answer back unless you want to say 'Yes' or 'No'. You are not allowed to defend yourself against his onslaught no matter how insulted or offended you feel.

You can if you wish, look to the magistrate for some form of support, or at least a little acknowledgement that the prosecutor is using his power of position against you. But if the magistrate has a reputation for a laid-back 'everybody's guilty' attitude, you're in big trouble.

And who cares? I call that abuse. What do you call it?

Then there is the nice policeman who yells through the door that if you don't open it immediately, he will kick the door in. Or the other nice policeman who withholds your medication while you are in custody until you agree with him.

Every day this form of abuse and much more is going on, and these are the people we turn to for help. When we feel threatened, how are we going to stop abuse if the system participates in it and condones it?

I must point out that these examples I have given you are not of a criminal on trial, but a witness of good character. So I am saying that abuse is alive and doing very well. Let's look out for it and remember that nobody has the right to

abuse you, no matter who it is. Report it. Stop it. Speak out about it. You don't have to have somebody scream at you or insult you. That's abuse.

And what about the statements that are obtained in police stations by intimidation, degradation, stand-over tactics, loss of civil rights and/or physical force? Are these things abuse or not? Who do we go to then? Another policeman perhaps, or ombudsman, a newspaper, a solicitor, Victims of Crime, the local member? Who? Well I suggest you go to them all, because according to the law of averages, one will be on the side of justice and against abuse. Honesty will then win over brute force, and people in power who use their position to satisfy their own sick perverted minds.

Don't be afraid. Any form of abuse must be stopped. We must educate the young people in a new, more acceptable way of living and to do this we have to show them that we will not accept any form of abuse by anybody. Let us take responsibility and stop passing the buck.

Somewhere, sometime, we have all seen some form of abuse and done nothing about it. Well, look in a mirror and ask yourself, do you approve of abuse? You will answer 'no'. I'm sure of that. So all you have to do is report it, and it will soon stop. If you have never done something about it before, it's not too late. Do it now if you know it to be true. Lives can be saved and people protected from those who use their power in this sick and distorted way. If you are asking yourself, how can I say such things about our legal system and our police, well ask no more. I will tell you.

During the course of my life I've had the sad but good fortune to have known a beautiful person who has had an addiction problem for some years. This brought me into very close contact with police and the courts on a number of occasions, and I have seen the abuse, felt the abuse, and witnessed the abuse, all while being innocent of any crime.

The sad fact is that many people will never want to believe that in our courts and in our police force, as well as our Christian clergy, there are people who need help themselves. Because they have a back-up system of co-workers to help cover it up, they will never be stopped or receive the treatment they themselves need. I am not trying to undermine these people or their work. But I am trying to say, let's get our heads out of the sand and admit that things are wrong everywhere. Not just in some of our homes.

I have learned the hard way to face it. Abuse in some form or another is everywhere, and the abuser doesn't have to look different from other people. Remember he or she can be wearing a uniform, or be very well dressed at all times. And may be very well educated, or not at all. They do not have 'Abuser' printed across their forehead, and don't always lurk around parks or toilets, although many have done so. What I'm trying to say is don't turn your head away from the people in powerful positions because you have been taught that they are above reproach. If they are human beings, then they can be abusers.

I shall try to go on now about what takes place when the questions are asked of me. Did I know Kate Leigh? the notorious Kate Leigh. Well I personally didn't know Kate Leigh to talk to but I did know of the this big fat dark haired lady who was Kate Leigh. I remember my mother talking about Kate, because she was a shop lifter I don't know why she had to be a shop lifter because she was making a lot of money out of brothels and sly grog because that was her game. Mark Foy's is where we used to see her. She would go into Mark Foy's and in those days woman (especially fat woman) wore bloomers, rather big knickers with a lot of elastic. Kate would put the stolen stuff down her bloomers, I knew about her and she knew about me. I didn't realise who she was or what it was about I only did what I was told. As for opening my mouth or making a comment or saying anything it wasn't on. Yes Kate was a fat dark haired lady. I suppose she's got some rellies alive today who might think she was as nice as a little girl going through hell. I just thought she was a horrible fat old lady who did nasty things.

And there was Tilly, now Tilly portrayed in the Underbelly series they tell me they made her look pretty or something and I said I've never looked at the movie or the books about her. I don't want to. But she wasn't pretty she was a horrible little squingy blonde who was a rough as bags with the filthiest mouth. I know that when she went overseas on a ship called the Himalaya my father's brother's son was the head chef on the Himalaya, it was sort of funny how a certain element always seem to mix for want of a better word.

Tilly was quite a nasty bit of goods and ran a lot of brothels and things.

As a young person I had my own fears, horrors and trepidations for what was happening to me, these were horrors within themselves. If I sound now like it's OK it's just a story, it wasn't then it was a real live horrible story and I was one of the star players you might say.

It wasn't that this was done to me every day in a brothel it was that I was there for those who wanted children and many, many, many people, 'men,' wanted children and in some instances they wanted even the grown woman to dress like children.

For Kate Leigh and the Tilly Devine's, say what you may, but I wasn't invisible, I was definitely there.

The horrible thing about all of this, is I was always made to feel guilty for the sins that other people committed. My punishment has been lifelong. Who would I ever trust. It seemed like the truth would never come out or it would come out too late. But it's one of those things. Someone else asked why wasn't this book brought out before, I tried to explain that it would never have come out except for another crime committed against me and the wonderful person from the Victims of Crime in the Valley. In the beginning I thought that nobody wants to print a story with only one survivor.

Who cares its history now but the whole thing is, life was bad for a lot of people and they did bad and stupid things.

There's no denying I was born in to the most wonderful country on earth but was also born in to the most cruel and sinful family. Though a lot of my views and feelings have altered it's not really possible to alter what has been nurtured into your brain, your mind and your spirit.

I'm trying to finish off this book because there is more, so much more but my editor said to me there's 'always more' and it would never end so you must end. Of course, write the next book about what happened as an adult out in the world out there.

Did it turn out to be a wonderful world was everything wonderful was it like a fairy story? No, no, no it was a horror story that continued in my life and people are entitled to know that it was only the beginning of more pain. Because Mary did not know that she was suffering or was in the right and did not deserve to be made to suffer more from peoples cruelty and lies and no understanding and never knowing how to stand up to the bullies.

So life was long and very painful. But she did survive. She became the hand that many people needed to hold on to. Her love and understanding of people and their pain has touched many. She lives with total recall where not a day passes that her vision of the truly horrific and painful past is not with her. But she shows the world how to live with it and how to live without drink or drugs, prostitution or cruelty.

I love Mary and very dearly and sincerely and I'm glad I'm her, but we're coming to the end of the first chapter in my life.

I certainly am aware that we live in a disturbed world and caution is the name of the game. But it would be nice if I could learn to trust people just a little, or at least feel secure in their company. Maybe one day in the distant future I will be able to look at people without waiting for some form of attack, or to be put down, or insulted. Maybe, down the line a bit, I may even have a little faith in the judicial system. Perhaps even a policeman. Remember nothing is impossible as they say, and it would be nice, I think. You see, there are still lots of emotions I have yet to experience and each day of my life puts me up there, where I am in charge of me now, and that means new ground.

Speak up, speak out, keep to the truth, and one day we will slow abuse down to a stop.

Once again I say, don't misinterpret what I have said about some members of the police and judicial system. Just look back to what I have written earlier about the judges who must make decisions that you and I want. At the same time, it may not be the right one. The judge has a grave job. I wouldn't want it for a million dollars, because if we don't have the answers, how can we expect somebody else to have them? I have seen the person who appears to be the guilty one, be the one who is not guilty and is telling the truth. And the so-called 'honest' citizen telling lie after lie very convincingly, all the time looking like a saint. Now what would you do? Well, the judge did the one thing I ask you not to do. That is, don't judge a book by the cover, or the innocent will go to jail and the guilty ones will go free. Check as far as you can and pass your information on to somebody who will know how to handle an investigation without prejudice so that we protect the innocent from situations like the one in front of that judge, who obviously forgot or did not know that when a person cannot speak, or present themselves as well as another, it does not always represent guilt.

As I know very well. After all, the people who were responsible for abusing me were well-spoken, well-dressed, and well prepared for any questions or hint of their guilt so that it would always be somebody else's fault, never theirs.

It would be a good idea to go to any courthouse in any area on any given day and sit and take note of the proceedings. Hear the evidence, see the magistrate or judge, watch the police, watch the witnesses for and against, if any other than the police and their witnesses. See the accused in many cases wearing prison clothes or perhaps the old clothes they were arrested in. See them having their civil rights refused by not being given clean clothes that most families bring to them to wear in court. Not to impress anybody, but in respect of the court. You will have to remember that not all of them have been proven guilty of anything at that point, but have been held in a cell until proven guilty. It is not always 'innocent until proven guilty' in our courts. Now comes the hard part for you. Try to judge if the person is guilty or not. Forget how the person looks, regardless of whether you think they look like a crook. Try to look beyond the good clothes and the appearance of the witnesses. And now you be the judge. Remember, if you make a mistake, maybe somebody who is innocent goes to jail. But this is the point. When you accuse somebody of something, look at all the evidence that you can possibly get and don't lie — not to yourself or anybody else — because you will then become as criminal as the guilty ones.

There is help available now. Don't mess up the chances of catching an abuser just because you want to do it all yourself. Be smart. Remember no-one has the right to abuse. Uniforms don't give you the right, position doesn't give you the right, religion doesn't give you the right, marriage doesn't give you the right, parenthood doesn't give you the right — and the list goes on. Never forget it. No one has the right to abuse. If you think you'll forget, just ask me.

The things I have spoken off are many but also there is much that I have not spoken off. Now at the age I am I must say that it is so important to learn to live with things that are so cruel that they are unbelievable to others. If you expect understanding and care from those that have not ever felt a small portion of these sufferings you will be very disappointed. But the effect of your own handling and understanding will carry you successfully and almost painlessly through your life, but not totally, because mentally it lasts forever. But of course outside show is what the world wants.

I have been told that the world wants people like me because I am gutsy, I have shown the people success against the odds, that I am survivor who knows what happened to me. When a crim now departed this world met me he thought I was gutsy, that of course was the infamous Chopper Read. I would argue with poor old Chopper and of course he wasn't right I'm not that tough. I met another criminal in Wacol prison where I went in a Victims module, I visited there and one of the criminals there said that if I was any tougher I would rust. He too was wrong as I have not gotten tougher. But in my 80's I really believe I am starting to rust quite a bit.

I remember when I got a letter from 60 Minutes, from the very wonderful gentleman of that time who wanted to do my story, I declined and was approached many years later again. But I didn't do it for many reasons which I will explain later in the next book. I had to be careful. When you are writing something very true you have to be careful, careful that it's not changed in anyway because once you change it, it's no longer that true story.

When I was young I didn't even have somebody that I could fall back on or an ally and sometimes you needed somebody. But my mother was not somebody I could fall back on because she was with the enemy, she was part of them. I never could get over the fact that my mother would visit with that horrible family that they married me into and know what her daughter had been going through. That does leave a funny taste in your mouth to say the least.

I would really like to say is that there is a lot more of this story. It's as nasty and brutal as it was when I was young because it stays with you. You must pay for it. When somebody is brutal to you there's a price to pay. Sometimes the perpetrator walks away, but the victim doesn't really walk away from it even though they become survivors, but they don't walk away from it.

In my life I have suffered physically from many things. My life was a bitter and nasty struggle but I must explain to you that there was a wonderful person that I met a Dr Stulzman, who helped bring my life back to assembalance of something in order. Also at that time I had un-diagnosed cancer. There were many wonderful doctors I would like to thank and among them is our very own surgeon Dr Nick Crampton, Dr Crampton works on the Gold Coast John Flynn Hospital. Ah what a marvellous surgeon and doctor. He has helped me. They operated on me a few times and he has helped me to live, stay alive. And his wonderful offsider Dr Crilly, anesthetist extraordinaire may I say, these two people that have helped me to stay alive, really stay alive. Dr Steven Stylian endeavours to protect me and care for me when things go wrong, lots of injuries to my body have haunted me through my life, the ones of course to my poor old head and neck.

When things happen and bones get broken they may heal but they leave old scars. There are many, many doctors that I can say are wonderful and without them I possibly wouldn't be here. Many, doctors have kept me on my feet, to stitch up, patch up and put back together. There are so many people for who I must say thank you and many people I can't say thank you to, many people I think about often as I'm sure they think about me. The rag doll, that they put together, the woman that didn't know how to eat without being sick. The woman who had so many problems, so many hang ups, so many phalluses, so many fears and then you put that smile on and out you go.

Another wonderful person came into my life a Solicitor by the name of Val Bellamy who I believe ended up in trouble himself. But at the time he knew me he said you must write and tell the country what happened to you. So that was perhaps the beginning.

At the beginning of the book my friend and solicitor Ralph James wrote a letter to be included in the foreword. I have known Ralph for many years; he is an accredited specialist in criminal law and a lecturer of criminal law at University. Ralph has contributed his learned opinions on the crimes and sentencing of the offences against me, Ralph is still a good friend of mine today.

Letter from Ralph James

Based on my experience in Criminal Law it is indisputable that Maria's parents committed a multitude of offences. Were they to be convicted today of the horrific sexual crimes they perpetrated against Maria the maximum penalty would be 25 years with a non-parole period of 15 years. But these crimes were committed in the 1930's and 40's, a time in Australia where capital punishment was a cornerstone of the criminal justice system. For their crimes, Maria's parents and others would have faced the death penalty for carnal knowledge of a child under ten. For a conviction of carnal knowledge of a child 10 – 17 years by a parent the penalty was ten years goal – and a whipping could be ordered by the judge.

These penalties are sobering when viewed in the context of this book. Not only Maria's parents and her three brothers but also every client in the brothel convicted of these crimes could have faced the death penalty. The sensational story would have been splashed across every newspaper in the country and the plight of the little girl so horrendously tortured would be known in Australia and probably worldwide. As it is, this story was hidden by a brave woman who could still find compassion to love her mother after suffering untold cruelty.

I have been aware for some time that Maria has been committed to writing an account of her life. Having read the book is much more than a story about torture, it is powerful and moving and tells of the triumph of the human spirit of a little girl and has been an incredible lifetime in the making.

Ralph James
Solicitor
Accredited Specialist - Criminal Law

So here I am saying I think I am coming to end of that first book. But we will know soon whether I really am. I hope the people who read it forgive me for being mis-mashed here and there but that's the way it was. The violence of people against me has died down but the violence to my body I must take to the grave with me. I hope that the people that read this book, those that will care about me and those that won't care about me, those that will like me, those that won't. Never the less I hope that perhaps from it, I give you the courage to stand up, stand straight, think beautiful thoughts and try to make things nice for everybody. In doing so, you make it nice for yourself.

I felt a feeling of helpless desperation, who would believe me? My parents, brothers, abusers, Kate Leigh, Tilly Devine, Police. Would they confess? And then one little sweet lady counsellor got if right; now I stand alone and the story goes on and on.

When I speak of this horror I do not cry for me, I cry for Mary.

TO MY BELOVED CHILDREN
Where are the little girls I carried
Who are those boys so tall
Wasn't it only yesterday I held their little hands
So that they wouldn't fall
When did my little girls become so beautiful
They were so tiny yesterday
Or is it my imagination
Could the years have passed this way
Where are the little arms that held me
The little wet kisses on my cheek
The beautiful big eyes at Christmas
That finally closed in sleep
Their love they said would last forever
Is now buried in the deep
If only I could show them yesterday was real
And the pain and the hurt from words they have said
Can't alter how I feel
And though my girls are now women
And my boys have grown to men
I love them all
And always will
As I truly loved them then

CPSIA information can be obtained
at www.ICGtesting.com
Printed in the USA
LVHW080007130821
695208LV00016B/937